Club Sandwich

Goes Great with Chicken Soup

Club Sandwich

Goes Great with Chicken Soup

A Collection of Best-Loved Stories
from Jess Moody

BROADMAN
& HOLMAN
PUBLISHERS

Nashville, Tennessee

© 1999 by Jess Moody
All rights reserved
Printed in the United States of America

0-8054-1828-8

Published by Broadman & Holman Publishers, Nashville, Tennessee
Editorial Team: Vicki Crumpton, Janis Whipple, Kim Overcash
Typesetting: TF Designs, Mt. Juliet, Tennessee

Dewey Decimal Classification: 242
Subject Heading: CHRISTIAN LIFE—ANECDOTES
Library of Congress Card Catalog Number: 98-55937

Library of Congress Cataloging-in-Publication Data

Moody, Jess.
    Club sandwich : goes well with "chicken soup" stories from
    Jess Moody / Jess Moody
      p. cm.
    ISBN 0-8054-1828-8 (pbk.)
  I. Title
  BV4517.M665   1999
  242—dc21   98-55937
                                                        CIP

3 4 5 6 03 02 01 00 99

Dedication

To our 3-D, technicolored grandchildren: Christopher Stephen, Sean Adam, and Jessica Amelia Moody. More fun to watch than riding the Big Spider at Six Flags. I pray for your next fifty years. You are loved. Follow Jesus and don't forget us!

"America needs a better philosophy. Our nation's best don't seem to be thinking these days. My whole life has been spent with the power of Story. Jess Moody is an American treasure—a combination of Paul Harvey and Garrison Keillor. He can capture in a story more truth than one could hope for. He is the only preacher who ever made a real dent in Hollywood. There are far more stories than he is telling here."

—Harvey Bernhard, motion picture producer

Table of Contents

Foreword

Randy Quaid is my brother, and we have a wonderful mother Nita Quaid. When she was about sixteen years old, she was a close friend of a young youth preacher named Jess Moody.

In those days, there was a great movement of spiritual power among the young people.

In the North, there was Youth for Christ, spearheaded by Billy Graham and others. Jess Moody was one of the others, and was present at the founding of Youth for Christ in Winona Lake, Indiana. Billy Graham and Jess traveled separately, but unitedly, for that organization.

In the South, there was the Baptist student awakening, and thousands attended in the major cities. My mother was one of those in Houston. The young preachers, like Jess, were almost like modern rock stars. Young people, by the thousands, thronged to hear them.

Years later, when Randy and I came to Hollywood to try to break into the movies, Mother said, "When you boys get there, be sure to attend Jess's church, The Shepherd of the Hills in Chatsworth, California." We did just what Mother told us to do, and Randy served on Jess's board for seven years.

We learned a lot about Jess, especially his Big Christ, his humorous normalcy, and his ability to tell stories.

Many people have asked Jess to write books of his parables, folklore, and just plain down-home fun.

At last, he has done it.

My wife, Meg Ryan, and I have a great affection for Jess and Doris.

I wouldn't be surprised to see a clamoring for more books by him—especially those filled with his stories from life.

Enjoy this Club Sandwich, along with a little chicken soup.

It should warm your heart.

It does mine.

Dennis Quaid

ONE

Mother's Last Date

"Burt Reynolds Dates My Mother!"

Sounds like something from the *Star* by the checkout counter at Ralph's Grocery . . . but that's exactly what happened!

Connie was dying of cancer of the brain. It was irreversible and soon coming. She had come to West Palm Beach on what she knew was her last trip. She wanted to see those grandchildren—Pat and Martha—and her son and daughter-in-love (as she called Doris) just one more time.

She came by on her I'm-just-dropping-by-on-my-way-to-heaven trip. That was exactly why she made the trip, and precisely how she had worded it.

Outwardly, Mother seemed as strong as garlic; inwardly, she was three weeks from the eternal journey. This outward mother fooled us, lulled us, by her wit and down-home humor, into not understanding the gravity of her illness.

In just three weeks, Connie would be sitting in her bed. Doris, Patrick, Martha, and I would come into the room, to be greeted with strange words to us, indicating that cancer had finally reached that strategic part of the mind:

"What a nice young family! Have we met? Nurse, please introduce them to me!"

. . . a knife into all our hearts; a pain, the intensity of which I feel piercing my soul even as I write this.

That is how she would soon be, but not as she was that night in Palm Beach in 1967.

Now, she showed great strength, great humor, and profound interest in her Patrick and Martha. No one is quite so enamored with children as a grandmother.

Now, she was reminiscing about Texas, about Burkburnett, Boom Town, and how she met Dad, and what a flirt he was.

She told about the wildcatters, fortunes being made and lost overnight, her experiences as a musician, her huge family, moving to Columbus, New Mexico, where they had to hide from Pancho Villa.

Her eyes danced as she spoke about being herded out of Oklahoma, with the small army of two parents, ten children, several dogs, two cats, and a milk cow.

There was fierce pride in these people who had some Cherokee blood in their veins. The Oklahoma Land Rush had sent ambition and greed, running rampant across those plains, taking all the land and dignity from the Cherokee Choctaw and other Indian people.

When the Mexicans were stealing across the Rio Grande into Texas and were laden with the terrible appellation, "Wet

Back," Mother would say, "America has always had the problem of illegal aliens, swarming across our borders. Ask any Indian."

Then the air would be pierced by her happy, infectious laughter.

These stories were just small shafts of light: jokes, puns, folklore songs, and poems that radiated from the limitless supply of lovely little witticisms, pouring out of her joyous mind.

One night in West Palm Beach, I snapped out of my sleep, thinking of Mother downstairs. Slipping into my bathrobe, I walked quietly to her room.

She was not there.

I had been warned that, at any given moment, when the cancer hit her memory, she might do anything.

I searched the house—no Mother.

Where could she be at 4:00 A.M.?

Finally, I checked the little porch outside her room at the pastorium, which is what Baptists call the preacher's house.

When I came out onto the porch, there she was, sitting in a rocking chair, wrapped up in a blanket, facing the intercoastal canal that ran in front of our house. There was a bit of a chill in the predawn night.

Mother looked more Cherokee than I had ever seen, wrapped in the blanket.

"My sister, the moon, is really doing her job tonight, isn't she?"

She was. The moon was pouring her liquid silver upon the water, cutting a light path across the Intercoastal.

The light path ran across the water in a direct line to mother, as if God were smiling on her lovely, but tired, face.

"What are you doing out here?" I love-scolded her.

Her voice was not strong. The cancer had done its deadly work on her vocal chords. She had to squeak words out, a kind of breathy wheeze, like a small child talking softly.

"I was just sitting here . . ." She wrapped the blanket more snugly about her. " . . . thinking of your sermon last Sunday. You said we should love God with our best."

She looked up at me. Her eyes were swimming with tears. Eyes haunted by death's nearness, yet still beautiful.

"I was thinking about what I had with which to love God. Dad is gone. Our money is gone. I have only our little house in Fort Worth—along with my memory pieces: pictures, trinkets, old furniture . . . and Dad's dumb old car. These things will be worthless when I am gone—or the day my brain gives up to the cancer. Trinkets without memory associations are just pieces of junk."

She shifted in her chair.

"It is time for Claremore, Oklahoma Reality. No poetry works when you are squared away with death."

She looked up at me. "Son, I love you. You are my preacher-son."

I raised a hand to her shoulder, to give her assurance. She semi-scolded me.

"Don't stop me by the unrealistic faith assurance that I'll get well. I'm dying. I'm hurting with a stabbing pain, a pain that has a mind of its own. You said last Sunday that I should love God with that which most occupies my mind."

She hushed my protest with an upraised hand.

"You asked me what I am doing out here at 4:00 A.M. I'll tell you. I was . . . was . . . just sitting here, loving God with my pain. That is the one thing that most crowds my mind, my pain. I was loving God with my greatest possession—my pain."

She looked up, toward the moon—and past it.

"That's it, God. I give you my pain."

Then she did something I had seen her do a thousand times when conversations got on the heavy side. I detected that little sparkle in her eyes . . . even by moonlight I could see it.

"Just think, Jess. I'll soon be with Jesus, all my friends. In a few days, I'll know for sure, for certain, more than all those professors you are going to hire at that new college. And there's one more thing . . ."

I knew her well enough to know that some kind of zinger was coming: "Just think! I'm going to that land where everybody is a Methodist!"

She then turned to me with a laugh, and said, "I have tucked you into bed all your lifetime. Now it's your turn to tuck me in."

I did that with pleasure.

Having put the blanket about her neck, I started to turn away. She gripped my hand tightly. In her little girl voice, since the cancer had hit her vocal chords, she prayed; and I honestly thought I was going to die on the spot because of her prayer:

Now I lay me down to sleep,
I pray the Lord my soul to keep.

If I should die before I wake,
I pray the Lord my soul to take.
I ask this for Jesus' sake. Amen.

That was almost the last private conversation I had with my mother. That next day was crowded with things we all thought we had to do. I had a noon board subcommittee meeting, the new college planning meeting (I had founded Palm Beach Atlantic College—now we were trying to get it born), the hospital, some counseling, and some practical stuff at the church.

Doris was occupied with children, housework, a Woman's Missionary Union meeting, and telephoning.

Mother sort of sat around, getting miffed if we stopped the work to worry about her. She kept on painfully puttering around the house, trying to help as much as she could.

About six, that evening, she announced that it would probably be best if she went back to Texas—maybe tomorrow. I thought it must have been something we said or did. Of course, it was none of that.

Death's cool breath was beginning to blow on the back of her neck. She knew she had to get back—and fast.

About seven, our doorbell rang. It was Burt.

There he stood. One hunk of a gorgeous hunk. With a one-rose corsage in his hand. I noted a brown Rolls convertible parked in front of the house.

"I have come to ask permission to have a date with Connie!"

"You mean . . . you mean my mother?"

"How many other Connies are here?"

Here was America's numero uno heartthrob, great beefcake superior, asking for a date with my mother.

Burt pinned the corsage to my bewildered Connie, whose flabber was gasted to the max.

Doris quickly put her shoulder fur coat onto Mother. (I still think Doris was in on this deal. She says, "That's for me to know, and for you to find out.") In what seemed a nanosecond, Mom was swept into the Corniche, down the lakefront, into the night . . . with Burt Reynolds.

"Do you think we can trust Burt with her?" Doris kidded.

"I don't know. You know how she is!" I counterkidded.

Two hours later, Burt brought her home, walked her to the front door, held her in his arms, and kissed her—right on the mouth!

After he was gone, Mother's eyes were shining.

"I just realized something."

"What, Mom, what?"

"Maybe in a few days, I'll be gone; but right now, I am certain that I'm not dead yet!!!"

Then she said, "How am I going to explain this to the girls at Riverside Baptist Church? Folks in Fort Worth will never believe this; but I'm sure going to tell 'em!"

It is this, and a dozen other experiences with Burt, that make my eyes flash when some legalistic Christian (If you can put those two words together, it's an oxymoron!) jumps me about my friendship with him.

Burt is not a super-Christian; but I do know, maybe better than anyone else, that he has a real heart to try to walk in the Master's stately steps. He fails.

So do I. Did you ever fail to live up to what He wants from you? If not, then you can criticize weak, young Christians if you desire.

If not, physician, heal thyself. Please don't shoot the wounded.

Two days later, a columnist wrote that Burt Reynolds was seen in the Petite Marmite restaurant in Palm Beach, having an animated conversation . . . with his mother!

Connie would have loved that.

TWO

The "Thou Place"

I love Jewish philosophers.

Why them? Because, if hard rationalism hasn't ironed out the Jewish mother from their brains, they are rather God-haunted and have enough holy history in them to give eternal perspective to their philosophies.

God bless the Jewish mothers!

Martin Buber was one of those (philosophers, not mothers!), who wrote of the "I-It" and the "I-Thou" relationship, and interpreted a relationship in terms of communication. What sort of response happens in me when I see, let us say, an inanimate object that has an experiential connection that it communicates?

That which I like, merely admire, or use, but with which I am not able to enter into a meaningful dialogue—is an "it." That, with which or whom I may share—receiving as well as giving—with which or whom I can meaningfully dialogue, is a "thou."

Paul Tournier enlarges on this concept by explaining that there are "it places" and "thou places." "It places" are instruments of use, without sacramental or spiritual meaning. They say nothing back to me.

A "thou place," or thing, is that which communicates memories, emotions, or experiences that are stimulating or precious to me. For example, the other day I was fumbling through a dresser, and found my father's glasses. The mere sight of them instantly brought tears to my eyes. The last time I saw him, he was wearing those funny, old fashioned, out of date, crooked-to-the-face glasses. They were a little silly looking, but they were of infinite value to me—to no one else on earth; but to me, yes!

That moment, exquisite and poignant, was a rich "thou place" to me. Why? Because I was viewed through them by the man who sired and loved me and believed in me.

I can see him now, stooped over that old-fashioned Remington typewriter, two-fingering it (as I am doing now!) and pecking out those marvelously crafted, though totally unpunctuated, letters of advice, and patient care.

Those glasses will always be a treasure to me.

This little experience prompted me to ask "What are the 'thou places' in my life?" Main Street in Littlefield, Texas, in 1938. The football field in Wharton, Texas, in 1942. The Rena Marrs McLean gymnasium at Baylor University in 1945; also Old Main and Brooks Hall. The once-open field, now the site of the First Presbyterian Church in Wharton (it was there that I knelt in my commitment to the ministry).

There are "thou places" all through the Bible. I can see Zacchaeus, as long as he lived, watering the sycamore tree. It was a "thou place" for him!

Surely, the lame man must have come back to the Pool of Bethesda to help others see that it was Jesus, not the pool's waters, that healed.

The woman whom Jesus met at the well must have frequented that site until she was too old, then had friends bring her. On her deathbed, I imagine that, among her last words were, "I wish I could go to that old well just one more time."

A "thou place" is a place of meeting—where you and God come into a place of communing relationship, where your "perhaps" and His "sure enough" first kissed each other. I have such places in my hall of memories.

The altar of the old First Baptist Church of Littlefield, Texas, is a "thou place" for me. There I was truly *met*—was deeply touched—by God. I was assured of His presence and solidly guaranteed that tomorrow was mine, that I was included, and that He had a place for me—a "thou place"!

Joe Grizzle was the pastor. Dr. I. E. Gates was preaching during a revival in that little church. My mother was playing the piano for the meeting. There was great excitement in the air, charged with help and hope. Dr. Gates really laid it on the line that night. I was the only one in the house to whom he was preaching.

"Life is short. . . . Eternity is long. . . . Sin is evil. . . . The blood is red. . . . Your heart can be cleansed. . . . Just believe in Jesus! . . . Come now! Come NOW!"

I felt a powerful internal blockage in my soul that kept me back at first; but the compulsion to meet Jesus personally, to be cleansed, washed in the blood—yes, to be saved—was all over me, in my heart, my lungs, my brain. It was THOU! THOU! THOU! everywhere!

The compulsion to be saved was so forceful, so absolutely essential, so deep that I was driven down the aisle, with tears of deep faith, great joy release, great unburdening of guilt. God really came to me that night. I was met . . . loved . . . forgiven . . . completely challenged . . . and redirected—all in one glorious experience.

I was seated with John Henry Chapman, Gene Clark, Robert Hammons, David Storey, and John Porcher—all of us were nine years old. There is a glorious camaraderie among nine-year-olds. They were from several different churches in town. When Dr. Gates came to the end of his message and extended the gospel invitation, all of us came forward to announce our faith in Christ.

Robert "Babe" Hammons and I were received into the First Baptist Church as candidates for baptism. The other boys later joined their own churches.

These boys, in my later life, would all be instruments of God in causing me to enter the ministry.

My mother joined the Baptist church that night, coming from the Methodists. O, what a glorious meeting time that was! Mother and I were baptized two nights later by Brother Grizzle. That old prophet from the dunes of the Dust Bowl said a strange thing that night.

"Tonight, I am baptizing a nine-year-old boy who will become a Baptist preacher!"

That slapped my flam doodle! There was not one indication at that time that I would think of such a profession. Some even chuckled at the thought.

The years came and went. When I was eighteen and living in another town, but with my heartstrings in Littlefield, I received word that John Henry, Gene, Babe, David, and John Porcher had all died in the war.

God came crashing through my psyche like a cannon ball through a crate of eggs, and that tragic sorrow became a telescope to give me the far vision of a world lost and needing Jesus. I fell on my face in an open field in Wharton, Texas, and wept away my surrender to do His will.

Now, fifty years later, while learned men and women, in a veritable bath of irrelevancy, argue over how many angels can dance on a pin, I still feel the glow that has never gone out— a glow that started in a little church, so long ago. My wonderful "thou place"!

When one finds his "thou place," he realizes the sense of being at home, with no need of further information, no desire to go anywhere else, because there is nowhere else that can provide the "thou-ness" of a place like the place of meeting— where you and God met—where righteousness and peace kissed each other!

Adam and Eve, in the Garden, were experiencing the "thou-ness" of place, never thinking of going anywhere else. When they sinned, they tried to hide from the "Thou;" but they couldn't. God sought them out and banished them from the Garden. Eden had become an "it."

From that time on, man became a wanderer, a seeker for a place of his own. Abraham could have remained in Ur of the Chaldees, amid comfort and urbanity. But no!

There was a force driving him from the elegant Ur because there was no place of meeting there, an "it place," to a land not of his knowing.

Abraham knew there was a "thou place" out there—somewhere—and when he arrived, he wasn't quite certain *where* it was; but he was certain of the "thou-ness" of it.

Better in a desert with a "thou" than in a palace with an "it"!

Moses and his hundreds of thousands made the big break out of Egypt, because Egypt was a clammy "it" to those people, called the Chosen People—or a people destined for a "thou place" with God.

They wandered for forty years looking for that "thou place"; and, when they arrived, it was confirmed in their hearts that they were truly—at long last—*home*.

"I must find my own place," our son told us, when he announced that he was going away to college, to Mercer University, instead of attending Palm Beach Atlantic College, of which I was president. He said more truth than he knew, because he was saying that he was searching for a "thou place" of his very own creation.

For Wesley, it was Aldersgate.

For Luther, it was Wittenberg.

For D. L. Moody, it was a shoe store.

For my mother and me, it was a little church revival.

For Billy Graham, it was a tent meeting.

For E. Stanley Jones, it was in Memorial Methodist Church in Baltimore.

Note what Jones said concerning that moment: "This time, I was deadly serious—I was not to be put off by catch phrases or slogans. I wanted the real thing—or nothing. No halfway houses for me; I wanted my home. . . . I had scarcely bent my knees, when heaven broke into my spirit.

"I was enveloped by assurance, by acceptance, by reconciliation.

"I had *Him*—Jesus—and He had me! We had each other. I belonged. My estrangement; my sense of orphanage, was gone."[1]

Years ago, Harry Emerson Fosdick, usually thought of as pretty liberal, called it "being a *real* person," as though none of us is really real until we find Christ and Christ finds us.

How will you find your "thou place"? By understanding that God has already gone to amazing lengths to help you find it—and will go farther in distance; and further, in intensity.

Once more, to the Garden of Eden.

Adam and Eve had reduced themselves from a "thou" to an "it," with no possibility of finding themselves, without God's help. Then God came in the cool of the evening—the very time of the day suggests refreshing, replenishing, renewal.

But note what God did not do. He did not call out, "Adam, where is 'it'?" Hear the God who just won't give up on us, as He called: "Adam, where art 'thou'?"

The lesson for all humankind is simple. Remember, God is seeking you. The Hound of Heaven is at your heels; and you cannot and do not want to get away.

Where is your "thou place"? What's the matter with where you are, right now?

You say hopefully: "But won't a 'thou place' be a place of beauty, a place of transcendent spiritual magnificence?"

Friend, any old place will do. Little is much, if God is in it.

I remember when I first saw Calvary, outside the city wall, in Jerusalem. I was climbing up a walk from the garden tomb. When I crested the little hump, and saw the Place of the Skull for the first time, I was shocked. By what? For one thing, there was no Steven Spielberg, no John Williams score to back it up. No angel choir. No intoning organ.

Instead I heard a song about drugs: "What go-oes up must come down. Spinning wheel, turning around!"

Brassy . . . Crude!

There, across the street from Calvary, was a discotheque: Young men in khaki shorts—one of them shirtless—dancing with girls in miniskirts. At the foot of Calvary!

Then, I heard the grinding of gears. My nose was invaded by the unpleasant odor of heavy diesel fumes. Below me, at the very foot of Calvary, was a bus station. People were pushing, shoving, cursing for a place in line, with no courtesy intended. A Mary Magdalene walked by, plying her trade, seeking a client. Two Arabs were screaming at each other, haggling over the price of some small item. I noticed a crowded camera shop, over next to the discotheque.

Suddenly, I was seized with anger. Rage went through my body. "Why doesn't the Christian world buy out this area, and make it into a beautiful, peaceful park?"

I challenged them loudly! Then, a second thought hit me: "No, It must be as it is." Because that is the way *it was*.

In the midst of commercialism, pleasure, sin, bartering, and rudeness, God raised up the greatest "thou place" of all time! With noise all around and counter currents swirling, hate broiling, and sin brewing, God came to us in reddened garments, courting your love and mine. He taught me that any place can be a "thou place"!

1. E. Stanley Jones, *Songs of Ascents*, Nashville: Cokesbury, 28.

THREE

The Trip to Bountiful

Dedicated to Sybil Goldsmith, who gave herself to the young people in a small town, Wharton, Texas. I have received several honors, from doctor's degrees to special citations; but none of them compare to the honor of sitting in her class, when I was a senior in Wharton High School.

She taught me to love the English language. Once, I was coming off the football field, and coach Howard Wade shouted, "Who missed that block on Kenneth Etie?" I answered, "It was me, Coach."

From the stadium, a voice rang out, "I . . . I . . . I—It was I, I, I, you idiot." Ever the teacher!

Her most famous student was Horton Foote, the great writer of the screenplay for To Kill a Mocking Bird, Tender Mercies, *and* A Trip to Bountiful. *Horton won an Oscar for each of these.*

Sybil was so proud of Horton—as well as all of her "kids." She lived a truly valuable life, and died a glorious Christ-honoring death.

I graduated from high school in Wharton, Texas. It was a chore to settle me down. I flinch as I recall the days when I was relearning that which my elders knew only too well, but were not able to teach me.

The trouble a teenager faces is his inability to see the whole landscape—the total picture. He seems able to see only his corner of the barnyard, and not the whole ranch. A young person needs someone whom he trusts to do the seeing for him. Usually, that person is not one of his parents.

That significant human instrument in my life was a tiny lady, maybe five-foot-two. She wore glasses with lenses like the bottom of a coke bottle, which magnified her brown eyes—giving the appearance that she could see right through you. The fact was, she knew the young mind so well that seeing through one appeared to be a given.

Her name was Sybil Goldsmith. She taught English.

But she didn't just teach it—she breathed it.

She never married; but she had a paramour—the English language. It was her daily bread, her evening star. She had only one goal: to make young eyes light up at the mention of Chaucer, Beowulf, Browning, Keats, Shelly, Wordsworth, and Shakespeare.

She wanted to produce people who could converse, feel, masticate, luxuriate, sense, and soar in the high cirrus clouds of verbal wonder.

There was no limit to how much time she would give to a truly hungry mind. Time and again, she said, hitting me gently in the midsection, "When something beautiful in the

English language really hits you there, you will then know the thrill of the mother tongue."

I made a speech in Mary Sanders's class (another wonderful teacher) about the death of a common soldier, buried in a foreign place, known but to God; and how the respectful little birds brought seeds to plant the grass and the flowers around his grave.

The birds, knowing nothing of war, did know that by his death the cannon ceased to roar, the green returned to earth, mothers stopped crying, daughters could find their lovers, little children could hug their daddys, and dads could weep unspent tears and swallow unnamed fears that Johnny might not come home again—but, thank God, he did! He did!

Hundreds of those man-boys were coming home.

Our fallen friend was not one of them, and a mother somewhere caressed his faded picture, and a father sat like stone in front of the fireplace—and thought of plans that died with his son, and hopes that crumbled when words tumbled from a young soldier-messenger's lips.

"All we know is that he is missing. No one knows where he is, sir."

But, as if an angel whispered it in their ears, the little birds knew; and thanked him for making the grass grow again—and the noisy guns to cease, and their horrid sounds live only in faint memories.

Now, only sweet songs of birds and the gentle breath of the wind in the trees make sounds in the forest where he fell.

The birds made a monument of green grass, encircled by flowers red, yellow, golden, and blue that stood like little soldiers guarding this revered spot where this revered man-boy fell—to never face having to kill another mother's son, whatever his race, whatever his native tongue. By his death, another lad lives.

Well, Sybil heard my talk about the fallen soldier. Squaring up right in front of me, and peering through the bottom of those "coke bottles," she said, "Don't you dare play with my soul the way you did in your speech. Darn you. I liked it."

She began to cry. And, as everybody in the world knows, it is a law in the state of Texas that old English teachers are not allowed to cry!

Sybil was as demanding of technical accuracy as a space scientist, but she did have a great heart for affirmation. When I am reaching for verbal definition in a sermon, there are three forces working on me: the Holy Spirit, the devil, and Sybil Goldsmith.

She produced many in whom she could justifiably take pride. But her brightest star is Horton Foote, one of America's greatest writers, winner of three Oscars.

It was Horton's longing to return to the memory haunts of that sleepy little south Texas town that prompted the writing of *Bountiful.*

The story tells of our inability to return to past social structures, past friendships, past "thou places," to search again for the wonder of other times and teenage memories. It is an almost impossible quest.

Jesus discovered this when He returned to His hometown, Nazareth. He stood in the pulpit and looked out at the "sea of the familiars," faces—each of which bounced back at him a memory, an experience, an old familiarity.

That happened to me. My first sermon in my old home church was a kick in the seat of my psyche.

The first sight that pierced my already unstable confidence was an old friend who knew me better than I wanted him to . . . and to whom I had owed five dollars for two years!

Then there was a girl, maximum pulchritude, for whom I had hankered—and she knew it—for years. Those knowing eyes pierced right through my ministerial confidence.

Then there was the hyper-fundamentalist barber, with the six-foot-long millennial chart, which hung in his shop, and which he slavishly taught to the prisoners in the chair.

I distinctly felt his eyes biting at me: "Oh, yes, isn't this J. C. Moody, the son of the man who ran Moody's Cafe and Moody's *liquor store?* I dare the likes of you to teach the Bible to me!"

I am quite certain now that none of them felt the way I interpreted the situation that first Sunday morning. But I remember the feelings of helplessness and absolute terror as I attempted to communicate what little I did know.

It may have been a similar social context that day when Jesus stood up at Nazareth—except that Jesus surely never felt the shaky confidence that caused my young hands to tremble that Sunday long ago.

He is confidence.

He had confidence that day—the congregation didn't.

"Isn't this the carpenter's son?"

The congregation in the synagogue that day had unhearing ears and unseeing eyes. Not a word from Jesus sank down into their personalities because of that massive insecurity that says,

"Nothing divine can come from anything with which I am familiar."

Like the woman from the hometown of the Wright brothers who said, "Man can never fly. Man wasn't meant to fly. If man ever does fly, it won't be anyone from Dayton, Ohio!"

Beware that you do not drown the miracle that God plans for your life, simply because you can't believe that miracles happen in Bountiful. Believe in the omnipresence of God, that He works effectively, even where you are—right now—living. Even in your very familiar home—even in you!

Miracles can come to Bountiful.

Sinai is more barren, less pretentious than Bountiful. The Ten Commandments were given to the world *there*.

Bethlehem was an insignificant jerkwater town, a watering place just outside Jerusalem. The *King of Kings* was born there.

The mountain on the shore of Galilee is still only a long slope of green, dotted with yellow and white daisies. The *Sermon on the Mount* was preached there!

Calvary's Hill is located on a limestone hump next to a din of noise from a bus station and a bar. All mankind finds eternal life there—right next to a bus station and a bar!

I can see some person asking directions in Jerusalem. "How do I get to Calvary?"

"Well, it's just two lights down this street, you turn right at the bus station, and it's right across the street from Harry's Bar! You can't miss it."

One day I was walking on the square in Santa Fe. I noticed a beautifully polished bronze plaque on the side of an old building: "Here at this very site, on August 13, 1907, nothing happened."

Santa Fe must have been a pretty boring place when sheer loneliness reaches up—and the high peak is *nothing happening!*

That was the mentality of Nazareth.

We will not allow anyone to break up that for which we are very famous, being a boring place. If they break up our reputation by causing something to happen, the only logical thing to do is stone them. That's what Jesus' hometown tried to do to Him.

He dared to inject the thought that the God of the universe could fulfill a major prophecy from Isaiah in Nazareth—before their very eyes!

Maybe in Lourdes.

Perhaps in India.

But not in *Bountiful!*

Perhaps most saddening of this tiny episode of the frustration of Jesus' power by local, hometown unbelief is that He was totally successful in all the tiny towns He passed through—but not in Nazareth.

> Poor Nazareth!
> Home of the Nazarene.
> Could have been
> The greatest little
>   Lighthouse
>   ever seen!
> But no,
> 'Twasn't to be.

They went their way
  unblest
  because
They closed their eyes
When touched
  by
    the Best!
        (Jess Moody, Paris '47)

Don't give us the blame!
Just the same, the lame, the tame.
We aren't interested in the game, the fame.
Just the peace, the anonymity, being quietly left
  alone.
Go somewhere else, Christ!
So, Jesus slips away and walks to another village
  beside some quiet sea.
Then one day, He came to my little town—and
finally,
  to me!
        (Jess Moody, Oslo, '49)

The problem in your Bountiful is not the ranting town athe-
ist, not the resident Bolshevik, not some institutionalized evil
in your city. The problem in Bountiful is that it is wed—in
conjugal, long-term, yawning relationship—with monotony.

They come to church, just as they are, sing "Just as I am,"
and leave just as they were.

Life is more than sitting around, witnessing the banana
pudding turn black, listening to ants eat, and watching the
grass grow.

FOUR

The Day I Slept
with the Pope

Pope John Paul II came to Los Angeles. It was an event that stirred the minds and imaginations of millions of Los Angeleans, including me.

I never knew the influence I exerted in Los Angeles until I received an invitation to be with His Holiness.

My ballooned *ego* burst when I realized he had invited four hundred other pastors to be with him *and me.*

I wanted to be there, deeply, but I had a problem. I was scheduled to preach in several different East Coast cities. It was a grueling, driving, draining experience. The tour included hard traveling, and at least three sermons a day. It was an Advil, aspirin, bone-aching, body-breaking week.

I arrived on the redeye from Chicago at 5:00 A.M. of the day the pastors were to meet with the Pope. The meeting was to be at 3:00 P.M. and the Pope was to fly directly to Dodger Stadium for a giant rally.

After arriving at our home and greeting Doris, I found things had really stacked up, so I rushed to the office, dealt with a couple of staff situations, two counseling sessions, and an overdue writing assignment that *had* to be finished.

By the time I was to go to the Pope's meeting, it was late—and I was famished, so I grabbed a big In-and-Out burger, some fries, a large Coke—and a *second* miniburger.

I *said* I was hungry.

So, I grabbed the diet food, swerved through L.A.'s grueling traffic, swallowed the burgers and fries, washed them down with the Coke and there it all lay, like a rock in the pit of my stomach.

Well, I hunched down between two of my good-friend pastors, Robert Schuller and Don Moomaw.

The Pope arrived midst pomp and circumstance, followed by the child giving a rose, a stentorian prayer by a priest, some greetings by the local politicians, and a very brief word from the Pope in English, garbled by a Polish-Italian accent but somewhat understandable, and certainly appreciated. Then came the program of various musical offerings to the Pope.

The first was a beautiful, gentle, sweet little rendering by a violinist. It was long—quite lovely, but long. The eyelids of the tired pontiff were almost at half mast by the end of this lovely presentation.

The next rendition was by a quite excellent flutist, whose gentle tones wafted over the air-conditioned auditorium. It was quite lovely, but lengthy also.

All of this, on top of the two burgers sitting rocklike in the pit of my stomach, began to do deadly work.

His Holiness and My Sleepiness were in absolute agreement. Just before my eyes lowered like the final curtain, I noticed that His Drowsiness had just about "lost it" also. Then I was mouth-open dead, basking in the arms of the goddess Morpheus—which means I was zonked out.

Now apparently the next number for His Drowsiness was to be quite unique.

The next item on the agenda was an African drum and bugle corps. There were drums as large as a king-sized bed, mid-sized drums, ten snare drums, twenty buglers, bells and lyres, and dancers of the heavy stomping type. And they were all smuggled onto the stage under my sleeping along with His Snoriness.

Then it came time for the presenters to begin. Three stood in front of their drums. As though by one giant signal, the muscled arms swung like sledge hammers. The thunderclap compounded by an earthquake multiplied by ten thousand shouts of archangels: **BARROOOMMM!**

I leaped straight *up*.

The Pope sat bolt upright.

"WOWOOH!" I yelled.

Bob Schuller turned his head away in embarrassment. Don Moomaw bent over double and laughed.

The Pope smiled, and looked in my direction.

I crouched down behind a lady with big hair, then gazed around as if to be looking for the culprit, "'Twern't me!" my look told the bewildered onlookers.

But "'Twas me!" I must confess.

I did sleep with the Pope.

FIVE

Rose Kennedy's Manger Heart

One of the scores of joys of being the pastor of the First Baptist Church of West Palm Beach, Florida, was becoming a part of the Palm Beach family.

The milieu, the sociological context, of the Palm Beach–West Palm Beach area must be understood.

West Palm Beach is the business/employee side of the larger community. The economic level is considerably lower than that of Palm Beach, which is the employer section of the area, as well as the residential district of retired wealthy, among them the major scions of America's greatest corporations.

Palm Beach is a haven of the rich and famous. As such, there are scores of reporters, photographers, and journalistic lookee-loos behind almost every palm tree. Scandals are exaggerated and overly reported. Some have no basis at all.

The most horrific scandal was the Chappaquiddick Bridge incident involving Ted Kennedy and Mary Jo Kopeckne. This was truly one of the most disturbing of all because it was such a mortal final straw for the Kennedy family.

The first tragedy was the midflight explosion killing Joseph Kennedy Jr. The second was the cruel assassination of President John Kennedy. Then, the shooting down of Bobby Kennedy at the Ambassador Hotel in Los Angeles.

Another was the loss of a daughter in a European plane crash in World War II. Another was the mental retardation, experimental operation, and final institutionalizing of daughter Rosemary.

Amidst this killing off of the firstborn, the second, and the third was Joseph Kennedy's stroke. I was at St. Mary's Hospital when Mr. Joseph Kennedy was brought in. We had prayer for him.

The next day, I revisited the Kennedy hospital room. Actually, I was in the hall—not wishing to disturb.

I met Bobby Kennedy coming out of the room. He was quite testy about something, uttering some profanities.

We had met before and he assured me that his anger was not directed at me, that it was something between him and Cardinal Cushing.

He never explained, except to say that he knew d— well that his father was in a deep coma, that he had not suddenly come out of it, and "he never would have said that." I always wondered what *that* was, but it wasn't my place to ask.

Bobby thanked me for my prayers, saying, "He needs all the Catholic and Baptist prayers he can get."

After the serial carnage and scandals, I felt that there was too little emphasis on the one person the whole world should have been comforting, *Rose Kennedy*.

Talk about grace under fire! I have seen Christians under the cannon, but none ever bore up more gracefully, or gave a more sterling witness for her faith than Rose.

I taught a Bible class at the home of Barbara Holmyard, the Champion spark plug heiress. Amy Vanderbilt called it the "Billion-Dollar Bible Class."

It was hardly that, and I never saw a penny out of it myself, nor would I have dreamed of doing so.

Princess Alexandra of Greece had been invited to come, and she did. And Rose Kennedy came with her.

When I saw that Rose was present, I immediately changed my subject for the day to "Christ Is That Sense without Which Sense All Other Sense Is Nonsense." It was a little homily on death.

The outline was "Three Attitudes Toward Death."

1. You can fight it.

2. You can take flight from it.

3. You can make a deal with God.

After the class, Rose whispered in my ear, "I made that deal a long time ago."

"You must tell me that story some time," I said.

"I shall."

She literally sparkled her faith all over me.

One evening I met her at a most inspiring occasion. Doris and I were invited to attend a special meeting benefiting retarded children. The children served the meal, and I might add that they served it beautifully.

Mrs. Kennedy sat to Doris's immediate left and I sat at Doris's right. After exchanging banalities for a while, I reminded Rose of her promise to tell me about the deal she had made with God long ago.

"I was a spoiled young bride of a very strong-willed man, a socialite who attended every function possible," she began. "We were expecting a child and were quite elated at the prospect. The day came when our child should come. She was a beautiful child. We were ecstatic.

"It wasn't long until we realized that there was something terribly wrong with her. We took her to the doctor who confirmed our fears. She was retarded, and nothing could be done."

I was amazed by one thing. The sparkle of living faith was still quite evident. It shone in her eyes and her total countenance.

"Some anger grew within my heart," she continued. "How could God do such a thing to this child—and especially to me? I turned my back on God, my husband, my closest friends—and became a recluse."

"I can imagine," Doris chimed in.

"But, there is more to the story . . . isn't there?"

"Oh, yes, much mo'ah." Her Bostonese was a 180-degree opposite to our Texanic-slow speech.

Mother Kennedy went on. "My husband and I seemed to shun the child. One evening a major event was happening in the city. I wanted to go, but I was so filled with wrath that I thought I might create a scene. My husband feared it, so we decided to just stay home that evening.

"I was boiling over with resentment. There was a lovely woman who was one of our maids. She sensed my boiling soul. 'Please excuse me, Mrs. Kennedy; but I've been watching you the last few weeks. I love you very much, and I hate to see this destroy your life.

"'I say this as gently as I know how: Mrs. Kennedy, you'll never be happy until you make your heart a manger where the Christ child may be born.'

"I fired her on the spot! You have no idea how filled with anger, how isolated, how focused on doubt I became."

As I sat and looked through this lovely transparency, I felt a rush of unabashed admiration. I realized that I was sitting with the greatest Kennedy of them all. But she was just beginning to open up. She was not only as clear as a window pane; she opened the window. The refreshing breeze washed our psyches.

It was at this moment that I was to experience a "Thou" moment, one of those existential exclamation points that becomes a soul-shout, and totally unforgettable.

Mrs. Kennedy continued, "That night, my mind ruminated relentlessly, keeping me awake until the late hours. I could not forget that lovely face, the sweetness of her countenance, the sub-surface joy that seemed to boil up continually in her spirit . . . and especially those deathless words: 'Mrs. Kennedy, you'll never be happy until you make your heart a manger where the Christ child may be born.'

"I have loved Christ all my life, and tried to be a good Catholic girl all my years; but this was one of those joyous moments of real *contact* with God and His Son. So I knelt beside my bed and prayed, 'Dear God, make my heart a manger where the Christ child may be born.' I felt a fresh new divine entry into my life, and there was born in me a passion, a love for retarded children.

"Oh, by the way, I rehired the lovely maid. She was with us for years, until her death."

Then Mrs. Kennedy lightened up with one powerful aside! "So, these children serving us here tonight are little messengers from God, drawing us all to His love.

"Oh, my, I *have* been talking too much. Would you please pass the salt?"

Jesus said, "You are the salt of the earth."

Rose Kennedy was, indeed, *that* to Doris and me that evening.

SIX

The Field of Dreams

As I write this, the fires have ceased in Malibu.

Homes have burned; our eyes have been riveted to the TV, watching in horror as nice people lost their possessions. My sense of admiration for the firemen could not be higher.

There is so much not to like—and to like—in L.A.

One day, you want to write it off as a conglomerate of goofballs, who think so weirdly that when something normal comes along, they make fun of it—as though decency, Christianity, churches, even the family are objects of scorn.

A city government, which seems bent on destroying the confidence of business, demonstrates an ignorance of and arrogance against the things that make for a successful city.

The city's leading problem isn't crime in the streets. It is crime in the bureaucracy. It doesn't take five thousand more policemen to resolve our situation. It takes about ten changes at city hall.

L.A. is a self-healing economy, if given only a few regular and slight governmental adjustments. Who couldn't love a state so beautiful, so naturally endowed, so filled with vistas that are ice cream to the eyes?

But, think about it.

Why would businesses be leaving a place where there are thirty million customers? Now, that's how I feel one day.

Another day, I see those brave, young firemen, with their faces, flintlike, against the red death roaring down Lopez Canyon.

You see hurting people bravely determined to rebuild their homes and their lives. And your skepticism fades away. And hope begins to surge within.

Now, it's Christmastime. We can use this joyous season to put our minds to the values that really count . . . to pray for strange people with strange, almost un-American ideas. Some of whom occupy high positions of power; some who terrify little people with their inverted bigotry and high-handed arrogance.

Decent people ask what a man asked of me last week: "Is it worth it to stay here and let my family be drilled with thoughts alien to the Judeo-Christian ethic by people who call good evil, and evil good?"

I had to think about that awhile. Then, I thought of a world that was just about like that two thousand years ago.

A ninety-five-year-old man named John wrote, "For God so loved the world, that He gave His only begotten Son, that whosoever believeth in Him should not perish, but have everlasting life. For God sent not His Son into the world to condemn the world; but that the world through Him might be saved" (John 3:16, KJV).

This Christmas, I'm praying that none of us will give up; but give in to the sweet message of the angels: "Fear not: for, behold, I bring you good tidings of great joy, which shall be to all people. For unto you is born this day in the city of David a Saviour, which is Christ the Lord" (Luke 2:10–11, KJV).

Several things I see in the Christmas story.

God loves the night. He thrills to put a diamond star in the darkness to tell people that, in spite of the darkness, the news is good, a Savior has been born.

God is so kind that He will not leave us to the varied speculations from nature worshipers, religious opportunists, and word-juggling philosophers as to what He is like.

In the darkness of night, He defines exactly what He is. He became what we are, so that the smallest child in a jungle can understand the gospel, when it is couched in a human being just like himself—with fingers and toes—the God who dignified every little human being on earth and became what we are!

God loves little-known people of average means. He didn't make the announcement to Big Shots. Not Herod. Not Caesar. Not Pilate. Not Caiaphas. Just plain shepherds. God loves the common person who is plodding along, trying to make a living and live a life.

God also loves nature. The greatest announcement of all time didn't come in a palace—or even in the Temple. It was out in an open field.

It was, indeed, the Field of Dreams.

God also loves little, helpless things. The Big Announcement came in a field of sheep, on a cool night. Probably the most defenseless of animals is a sheep. The shepherd had to stand close by, to take the *rod* and beat away the attacking wolf or the striking serpent; he had to take the *staff* to retrieve the frightened, fleeing sheep. Then, the grazing, smitten-by-serpents sheep are held by the tender shepherd, who *anoints their heads with oil*, putting on the best medicine available at the time.

Christ is the great Shepherd, who stands between us and the enemies of our souls, who holds our heads up when we are deeply wounded, and puts on the healing oil of His Spirit.

The sheep didn't understand what happened that starry night above all nights. Neither did we. But now we know. God knows. It is because of our Shepherd's care that I love this crazy town. God loves it too. Let's all turn back to Him.

After all, it's *Christmas!*

God rest you!

SEVEN

The Man with the Golden Eye

I had heard that there was a certain man in Hollywood who wielded great influence because of a singular gift, a talent possessed by very few people on earth: his eye. This man's gift was heaven or hell to the future career of every actor he met.

They said that in a New York minute, he could tell if an actor could make it or not; and this was not based on the actor's talent but on a characteristic very superficial to most people.

Many times, when the casting directors could not make up their minds between two actors for a major part, they called in "The Eye" to make the decision. One brief look and "The Eye" would say, "This one; not that one," and that settled it.

"'The Eye' decides," they said.

During the Bush-Clinton campaign, this man said, "Clinton is overladen with faults; his wife may be angel or devil—it doesn't matter. Clinton will be elected, because the camera absolutely loves him."

He said the same thing, with reservation, about Nixon. Nixon will be elected or defeated, according to what the camera says about his opponent. "The camera, in an unusual way, likes Nixon or hates him, according to the milieu, the swirling environment. His face says 'integrity' under one circumstance, and 'crook' under the other."

One face says, "Oops, I got caught. Sorry, Mom, I won't do it again." Mom crumbles. "What are you going to do with a boy like that?" She smiles, forgiving him.

"Another kid does the same thing and wails out repentance, and she beats him within an inch of his life. It's all in the look," the man with the golden eye says.

I had heard of this man, but never knew his name, or much about him. I wondered what he would be like, this genius, and longed to meet him. I could imagine him living in some plush Malibu Palace overlooking the ocean.

One Sunday, I preached a rather ordinary sermon on Jesus' gift of seeing in people what most people couldn't see. What he saw in Peter, James, John, and Nathaniel.

When we extended the invitation, the "altar call" as they call it in California, a man and his wife came forward. He was weeping. She was an attractive lady. He was a sartorial disaster. Blue jeans slit at the knee—then the fad of sixteen-year-olds (but this guy was forty-five), a faded denim shirt, no socks, and loafers. Hair, generally uncombed, and reaching his shoulders like a superannuated hippie, one that didn't turn Republican, like the rest of them.

"I really want to settle it with Christ. Right here. Right now." He meant it. I knew it. His wife knew it. We all knew it.

His name was Don Phillips. His father was a Baptist minister in New Jersey. We had met on a trip to the Holy Land. He and his godly wife and I had enjoyed each other's company on this trip, and they had requested that I pray for their son in Hollywood.

Little did I know that Don Phillips—the superannuated hippie—was "The Eye"!

Don Phillips has discovered a dozen famous actors and is known and respected by the cream of Hollywood's elite. We developed one of the most joyous relationships. Real friends. We would call each other late at night. Inconsistencies abounded.

"Jess, my dear pastor friend. I am sitting here with Randy and Dennis Quaid. We want to know what book in the Bible tells that the Messiah must die before the temple is destroyed."

"That's in the Book of Daniel."

"DANIEL! THAT'S IT! I'M RIGHT! RANDY, YOU OWE ME FIFTY BUCKS. WIN. WIN!"

You could hear him for ten blocks when he was excited.

As time went by, the man with the golden eye grew more and more into spiritual maturity. His wife, Dottie Pearl, a masterful makeup artist who won many awards ranging all the way from *The Texas Chainsaw Massacre* to *Tootsie* with Dustin Hoffman and Jessica Lange, finally left Don, and the marriage was lost in the sea of Hollywood relativity and the mud of misinformation. Don was quite broken over this, but I never heard him criticize God or the church even one time. He shouldered it like the true man he was becoming. This man had more demons to fight than the uncomplicated average Christian. He was like a referee in a prison football game; he had to make some tough calls, with threats from both sides if he didn't call it right.

The movie industry is laden with a hundred Judases ready to deny you and sell you for thirty pieces of silver. There are dragons behind every place a contract lies on a table. Gargoyles lurk on every casting director's couch. Phantoms twist every camera angle. Imps leap from ink wells of every Hollywood accountant's marking. Satan's copilots would sacrifice their mothers for more shekels to come falling on their heads.

This was Don's swirl-world. Any outsider who thinks he understands Hollywood also believes that purple bird dogs fly. It is a world not unlike the lottery, where one wins and thousands lose; and the only time people pray is while waiting for an audition or screen test.

I can't forget the casting director, Bobby Knight, speaking at our little theater group, dispelling the myth of who tries to get whom on the casting couch: "All your life, you have heard about the lecherous casting directors promising parts to the young beauties for couch-favors. It is with deep regret that I must tell you that today a casting director would not think about interviewing a young lady without a witness.

"Half the time, the girl will offer to do anything, *anything* for a part. Setups abound everywhere. They come in crying, 'Please help my son. He doesn't have a father since our breakup. Would you just come to my house and spend a little time with him?' When you get there, you are in the spider's lair."

This has happened many times. This was Don Phillips's world. He could write a book that would melt a hit man's heart. But "The Eye" continued to climb, to fight for his soul. He became a member of our church's board of trustees, a major assignment, and he served for eight years with great credibility and distinction.

One night, Don asked to take me out to dinner after a board meeting. Once seated in the restaurant, he opened up on me. "Moody, I am about to give up on you!"

"Why?"

"Because you have been trying to get this big, blind church to move out of this sure-death location for five years. They keep on balking, and you haven't the guts to put your job on the line for it. This church will do what you lead them to do; but you are afraid you will offend somebody. You are a nice guy, and you know where nice guys end up!"

Don was steamed.

"I want you to help me find out what to do." I meant it.

"I want you to get off your ordained butt and go find us a piece of property!"

"When do you think my ordained butt should go look for this property?" I asked.

"Tonight! We're getting in my car and we won't stop until we've found it!"

We drove till nearly dawn. Nothing.

"OK, there is a choice piece out there. Let's pray that God will get this cleared up this week."

"This week? Don, we've been looking for four years."

"OK, God, I'm sick of all this dillydallying around. This week! You hear that, God—THIS WEEK! Now, get to work, God. Enough of this STUFF."

Two days later, I was contacted by a realtor. The rest is history; but it was Don Phillips who made me get off . . . my . . . where I had been sitting on the premises and started me standing on the promises of God.

EIGHT

The Day Lenin and I Handed Out Tracts

There was a time when I was exasperated when I saw someone give out gospel tracts, those little pamphlets with a mini-message. I considered it gauche, a graceless, awkward way to witness.

There had always been a feeling of mine that one should build a relationship with another person before sharing something so deeply personal as one's faith. I have since come to believe that this is Satan's way to cause a carnal, half-committed Christian to have an escape hatch from talking to anyone, ever, about Christ.

Now, mind you, I have a deep aversion to the boorish sort of person who figuratively, if not literally, puts his knee in your chest and gets into your face, then—with halitosis breath—breathes out, "Brother, hhhar you saved?"

I put that group in a class of hot gospelers who mistake Jesus' words, "Let your light shine before men" for "Let your blow torch blaze before men." Often, they do more damage than good.

I was using my revulsion against such as a way of winding my way through society in as inoffensive manner as possible—and, as a result, I was a hale preacher well met by the town's nonseekers—until one morning.

I was having breakfast with a lovely, highly intellectual and stimulating Christian friend. It was his day to buy breakfast. When he left the tip for the waitress, he left a rather inoffensive little tract entitled "Here's a *Real Tip.*"

I asked him about it and he gave me a packet of them. "Hand these out—but always leave a generous tip. No nickels and dimes with your witness."

I put them in the glove compartment of my car—and left them there for several months. One day, Doris and I were in Louisville and stopped by a nice little restaurant on the west side of town for an evening meal.

I was fumbling through my glove compartment, looking for something or other, and I took one of the tracts, thinking, "I'm here in a place where nobody knows me. I'll drop one of these with this waitress." I felt like Savonarola or Joan of Arc—such bravery! After the meal I plopped down a tip, along with a "Here's a *Real Tip.*"

You will not believe what happened. Seven years later, Doris and I were in Louisville again, having dinner in the Brown Derby restaurant—in another section of the city.

While placing our order, I kidded the waitress and during my patter, mentioned something about being a pastor from Texas. When I said "Texas" she changed her demeanor and immediately asked, "Were you ever in a restaurant in west Louisville, and did you leave a little Christian pamphlet entitled 'Here's a *Real Tip*'?"

"Yes, I did." I remembered it quite clearly. Doris remembered it as well.

The waitress began to weep. She broke protocol and sat down at the table with us, asking a fellow waitress to cover her tables for a moment.

The story she told was an unbelievable story. She was cleaning up our table, took the tip and the tract, and read it. She was not a Christian, her husband was not a Christian and had told her that morning that their marriage was over. She read the tract, the words from Scripture convicted her heart, and she turned her life over to Christ. She went on to say that she took the Tip tract to her husband and *he* was converted. They were reconciled and were baptized into a local church.

"I cannot thank you enough for giving me the words I needed at the most difficult moment in my life," she said.

From that moment until this day, I have been an avid advocate of giving out little inoffensive tracts that quietly witness for Christ. I have had some wonderful experiences doing this.

Doris and I were given a trip around the world by Bob and Florence Turner, who were members of our church in West Palm Beach. We traveled to some of the most wonderful places on Earth: London, Paris, Berlin, New Delhi, Burma, Hong

Kong, then Tokyo. The Turners were royalty to us and included us in the royal family by their hospitality.

One of the prime destinations of our trip was Tokyo. The reason was that the city was hosting the World's Fair—and it was magnificent. We loved visiting the American Exhibit Building, which included the space capsule flown by John Glenn.

When I was the president of the Southern Baptist Pastor's Conference, John Glenn spoke when we met in Dallas and gave a glowing Christian testimony for his faith in Christ.

An interesting sidebar to the story. Our son, Pat, was a page for our conference and rode in the car to pick up John at the airport. For some reason, Pat had a terribly painful neckache. When John Glenn discovered that Pat had a neckache, he said, "I can fix that." He told Pat to put his head in his lap, and the great, world-renowned astronaut rubbed Pat's neck all the way back to the convention center. Pat didn't wash his neck for three weeks!

Now, back to Tokyo. Another item of intense interest were the moon rocks. We then went to the Russian Exhibit Building. It was packed with communist propaganda: glorious cities being planned, space accomplishments, and many items of interest. But what kicked my imagination the most was a magnificent statue of Lenin. It was a glorious tribute to the ability of the sculptor. It stood at the entrance of the building in overwhelming magnificence. The cause was, of course, the pits; the art was enviable.

Lenin's cape flowed gloriously, his cap sat in the most flattering position, determination clearly in his countenance, and one of his hands was outstretched quite appealingly, extended at the people level. I fixated on the hands as I always seem to do when observing a sculpted piece of a person. They were terribly appealing, and received my praise because all sculptors acknowledge that hands are the more difficult to do.

I have a mischievous streak in me, a legacy from my fun-loving mother. As I stood at the very entrance of the Russian exhibit into which hundreds of thousands of people cascaded right by Lenin's statue, the thought exploded in my mind: *What a great place to witness for Christ.* It was akin to charging hell with a squirt gun, but it was appealing, nonetheless.

I remembered that the arm bag that Doris carried was loaded with the gospel tract "The Four Spiritual Laws." With eagerness and veiled glee, I opened her bag and extricated a large fistful of the tracts. I then turned to the intriguing hands and made an amazing discovery. The tracts fit perfectly between Lenin's fingers. So, I placed one copy of "The Four Spiritual Laws" between Lenin's outstretched fingers.

The first Japanese visitor who came by eagerly seized a tract. So, I continued the process until our supply was exhausted. I personally handed out the last four tracts.

Therefore, I am the only person on earth to "persuade" the founder of the world's largest exporter of atheism to become a highly effective distributor of the gospel of our Lord Jesus Christ.

Bill Bright has sent out thousands of teams of witnesses. But none so effective as Vladimir and Jess.

NINE

Tripod, the Smiling Dog

Our daughter, Martha, is a dog nut. She never has less than two, usually three. I have never paid an ounce of attention to any of them, except to yell at them to stop being under, on top of, beside, behind, or over something—whatever it was. She did have one little dog who caught my attention. His name was Tripod. He had three legs—lost one while chasing a car.

He got around OK; acted as if he were born that way. But the thing about Tripod that struck me most was the way his mouth formation revealed his teeth, making him to appear to be smiling all the time.

To see this three-legged, gimpy, unidentifiable-by-breed mutt, hobbling all over the place, smiling, smiling, smiling, nearly drove me to distraction. It also inspired me in a strange way.

"I'm crippled, but I'm smiling, smiling, smiling," he seemed to convey. Watching him run to Martha, with all the love in his inspiring face, beaming up at her inspired me to write this little piece about all dogs.

I never knew a dog who possessed even one talent. I never heard one of them sing an aria from *Aida*.

I never saw one in a ballet from "The Dance of the Sugar Plum Fairies." But a dog, a good dog, has something that goes beyond talent—a good dog has the innate ability to be a happy, loyal friend.

Several things I have noticed about dogs. For one thing, well-bathed, well-fed dogs are not as creative as outdoor dogs. The outdoor dog is more creative because he has been blessed with the solid stimulus of fleas. House dogs are less realistic, more idealistic.

Have you noticed that idealistic people are idealistic in direct proportion to how far they are away from the smelly peskiness of life. They say that man is made in the image of God, which makes one feel sorry for God.

I believe I see more godlike qualities in a dog: everlasting faithfulness, quick obedience, ready repentance, consistent love, and short-termed anger.

Man needs church, Bible, Mother's prayers, and a dozen other spiritual stimuli just to keep him halfway straight. A dog has none of these and gives the world a good, steady example. Did you ever hear of a dog who betrayed a secret?

Dogs aren't stupid, either. They always operate on OPM—other people's money. Did you ever hear of a dog who *paid* for dog food? He never has to prepare his food . . . so he has his own private chef. And did you ever see a dog who washed or dried the dishes, made a bed, or took out the trash? He never cleans up the house, but sometimes he can leave the most repulsive of messes, and seldom get reprimanded for it. He has messed on the floor, and his nitwit master says, "Poor Fred. He must be sick. This is so unlike him!"

I never knew a dog who was hostile toward facts—in fact, he is generally and consistently apathetic to them.

Men are born to lie. Dogs are born to lie around. Lying hurts people; but lying around never hurt anybody too much.

Look what men and women do to a newspaper. They spend hours reading the front page, the sports page, the business section, the cooking section, or the fashion section.

A dog doesn't give a hiccup about what the president, or congress are doing. He doesn't give a bark in the night about who wins the Super Bowl. He does to a newspaper what ought to be done. The nearest thing to having a preference for any particular section of the paper is that surveys indicate that he prefers to use the editorial page.

The only critics he has are flies, and his tail swats them while he blithely lies around contemplating on very little. He has no money nor need for it. Perhaps he realizes that it costs too much to get it, and complicates everything too much to keep it.

Did you ever cogitate on the profundity of the fact that the only ones who were happy on both sides of the Iron Curtain were dogs? They could survive with or without communism.

No one ever shot him for crossing the border—and he never had, or needed, a passport.

A dog never climbed the social ladder—or felt that he needed to. The only time he ever climbed anywhere was when there was a bone up there . . . or when his master beckoned him or her up into the master's lap.

Also, you never saw a lunatic asylum for dogs. You never heard of a dog who was taken away by the men in white coats because the dog couldn't adjust.

And did you ever hear of a dog who was fired for not doing a good job of being a dog? In fact, he just lies around, doing nothing, and everybody praises him for it. He lies there, looking a little bored, rousing only occasionally to con you by licking your hand. If the facts were really in, perhaps dogs licking people's hands may have cured more neuroses than all the preachers and psychologists combined.

Dog food costs less than counseling fees. Everything comes to the dog who gives the impression that he hustles while he waits. And sometimes a dog can do as much good for you as a nurse; because he seems to know that most diseases get well sooner or later, no matter what you do about them.

Man attaches a great deal of meaning upon that which he pontificates, as though the stars would fall if he didn't get to express his ideas. Man speaks as though his comments will do some good. He intones banality, and then makes it a doctrine—or better, a DOGma. Dogs bark just because, without commentary.

Dogs aren't critics. I never hear one of them say, "I don't believe I would have worded it quite like that." And they seldom leave the room, even when bad singers sing. And, on certain high notes, a dog will sometimes correct you by hitting the note as it ought to be. But, generally, they are incurably apathetic to talent—and nontalent.

Dogs aren't socially inclined. They can get along with the crème de la crème. The Astors would throw us out of their mansion if they caught *us* licking off the floor. Dogs can stay in Trump Towers—at no cost—in spite of the fact that they can't eat with a knife, fork, or spoon. They can break wind in Buckingham Palace, and not even royalty will raise an eyebrow.

They don't have to have been born in a log cabin to become somebody, because becoming somebody is not a goal to be desired, and the only way a dog can become somebody is to be just a nobody who loves you.

You never hear of a dog who made a fool of himself, because his goal is not to impress. Only those with goals make fools of themselves, trying to reach the goals.

A dog is a stoic and is more consistent in his stoicism than his master is at being a Christian. He never worries about which came first, the Greeks or the Romans. In fact, he doesn't care if there ever were any Greeks or Romans.

He copies nobody. He is an authentic original nobody, and nobody can be nobody better than he. If he could seriously put his mind to anything for any worthwhile purpose, he wouldn't be a dog—and that, to him, would be the worst of fates.

He is better off than man because he doesn't need a constitution, bill of rights, government, judges, a half million laws to keep him on an even keel at being a good dog.

He is never sued for anything. In all the history of jurisprudence, no dog has ever been sued. If he ever does anything radically wrong, they always sue his master. Some people have actually been placed in jail for something their dog did. It makes sense to the dog.

And, if his master *is* put in jail, his master's wife may leave him; but his dog, who caused the incarceration in the first place, will wait for him. The dog will be greatly loved for waiting, and be rewarded for being a faithful old friend. . . . And all the while, he—the dog—caused the whole thing!

Now, who is smarter than whom?

And did you ever notice that no one ever criticizes a dog for not taking a bath? They criticize the master for not *giving* him one! People *take baths*. Dogs are *given* baths.

A dog doesn't have to get into the bath water. He is *put* there. He never has to soap himself up. It is done for his majesty. He never dries himself. It is done for his majesty. The only thing he does is shake himself off . . . and get the soap all over his master—and in his eyes. And everyone laughs and thinks it's cute.

Who's in charge here?

A dog's philosophy of life is, "You live your life, and I'll live mine—unless I need you." And did you ever notice that a dog never tells you what to do? He doesn't leave notes on the refrigerator. He doesn't nag disapproval. He wags approval. He is totally positive in his attitude. He is the Robert Schuller and the Norman Vincent Peale of the animal kingdom.

He doesn't go on walks. He is *taken* for walks with and by his master. He doesn't do anything—his master does it all for him, which causes one to begin to ask a pregnant question: Just who is master and who is dog here?

For whom is this walk being taken? Is this a pro-dog or pro-master walk? The master seems so fretful, so distracted, so troubled, so in the slough of despond. Poor thing! He needs to unwind. So dog turns this thing around and walks him!

Dog leads master throughout the park, stopping only occasionally for dogdom rituals of sniffing from bush to bush to make certain he is not infringing on somedog else's bush. When the taking-out-the-master-for-his-depressurization walk is finished, the dog knows to act quite exhilarated, leaping about and putting his paws on his master's knees, as if to say "I hope you are feeling much better now. Was it good for you? It was good for me!"

A dog truly loves that beautiful master because there is no love greater than the love of a dog . . . for food. The *universal dog* will kill, and even die, for the one who goes to the store, buys, brings home, opens, and prepares that glorious *food*.

A dog is like a lot of old men I know. When he barks, you think he is angry about something, when actually he is just clearing his lungs.

It doesn't take a lot of research to notice—have you ever observed this?—dogs don't engage in commerce, the business of trade. No dog has ever died of ulcers from watching the Dow Jones Industrial Average or NASDAQ. There is no recorded case in history of a dog jumping out of a building because of a stock market crash.

A dog must often wonder, when his master commits suicide: "Why wasn't he mature enough to handle it? Why couldn't he trust that heavenly Father he was always talking about? My master always provided food for me. I never had to worry about it. He must have worried too much about his great Food Provider. That's why he jumped.

"He jumped because something had eaten up his reason for not jumping. Now, he's dead, and he has lost his best friend—me. And I have lost the best food provider a dog could ever have!"

And when he is old and stifle displacea—which food providers call arthritis—stiffens the joints in his legs so when he raises his leg up to a tree, he falls over, . . . it is indicators like this that let him know the end is near.

At the end, the dog can only look at his new master and let the eloquence of his eyes pain-out the message of his deep hurt. The saddest part is to see the old fellow clumsily trying to play with the children, as he had done when he, too, was but a puppy.

Then, one morning, they find him with the old ball he would never trade for any bone under his paw. . . . his face flat on the floor . . . and sightless eyes, glazed, and facing the fireplace.

TEN

Friends

I have always been choosy about women. I don't know where that comes from, but it dates way back before kindergarten. I know it precedes kindergarten because it was there that I precipitated a crisis.

It took place the first day. Mother was teary-eyed, and I was an emotional wreck (as much as a kindergarten kid can be an emotional wreck), because Dad, Mother, Aunt Zetta, and Uncle Bruce had kissed me good-bye a hundred times each. I was the droolee.

No one can imagine what it does to a kid's ego to be told over and over, "My little darling is going to school!" I felt like Beau Geste going away to the foreign legion. I could almost hear the drums and trumpets as I was kissed farewell again and again.

Mother drove me not only to distraction but also to the First Christian Church, where the grand occasion took place. Mother took me into my class and I was seated in my place.

She kissed me—again—and walked out, crying. In about five seconds, I came roaring out of the room and ran to Mother.

She took me in her arms and said, "Be brave, darling. I know it's difficult. It will be all right. You'll get used to kindergarten."

Mother loved to tell about my response.

"Have you taken a look at that teacher? She is *ugly*! If I'm going to school here I don't want to look at her all year long. Get me in another class or I'm not going!"

They put me in Miss Emma Ruth Jones's class. She was the town prize, a real knockout. I took one look at her and said, "That's *much* better!" I could have gone to school there the rest of my life, so long as Miss Emma Ruth Jones was teaching. I was in love.

The experience of kindergarten is designed to teach a child social interaction. I was an only child, so it wasn't a success at first. I wanted what I wanted, when I wanted it, and where I wanted it—never mind who owned it or why I wanted it. It was Fist City if they didn't yield it up to my grubby hands. I was totally democratic—I fought them *all*.

But there was one kid who could handle me. His name was Robert Adams. He was friendly and playful. I liked him a lot! We were close and even spent the night together a time or two. Robert taught me how to catch a ball, I mean *really* catch it— any kind of ball. Robert and I seemed to be extensions of each other. He could scoop it off the ground, catch it in a leap, every way there was to catch a ball. His timing was perfect.

One night, when he was staying at my house, we talked about what we wanted to be when we grew up. Robert wanted to be another Babe Ruth. "I'm going to practice until I am up to perfect. Then when I'm about seventeen years old, I'll walk in and tell the Yankees, 'I'm here.'" He would do that. I was sure of it.

The next day at recess, he and I were playing catch. I was getting the hang of it, but I couldn't throw straight. After a few muffed pleas, Robert yelled, "Come on J. C., hit me in the hands!"

I was determined to hit the small target of his cupped hands. I threw it with all my might—it flew far over his head.

"My fault, I'll get it!" I yelled.

Robert paid no attention to me; he whirled around in hot pursuit of the little white ball. I was so embarrassed by my bad throw that I started running for it too. Robert was just a few feet ahead of me. Out of my quarter vision, I saw the truck. Robert didn't. A sickening *thud*. Robert Adams was dead. The truck driver had not seen him.

"J. C.!" a little girl screamed, "If you hadn't overthrown him, this wouldn't have happened." She kept screaming it with a high, irritating screech, "If you hadn't . . . this wouldn't . . . !"

I didn't know what to do. I ran home. With every step I could hear her. "J. C., if you hadn't . . . , this wouldn't have happened. . . . J. C., if you hadn't . . . , this wouldn't have happened."

I slammed the door, ran into the kitchen, and I froze in front of Mother.

"I just killed Robert Adams. I didn't mean to throw the ball away. Wanda Jean said I did it! She is right! I did it! I didn't mean to, but I did it! I did it!"

Mother took me back to the school to try to understand what had happened. Mr. and Mrs. Adams were there. I couldn't look at them. Mrs. Adams came over and knelt down beside me. "J. C., it wasn't your fault. It happened. It was God's will."

I could have kissed her, but I didn't like the God who took little boys' lives. I didn't go to hear Brother Grizzle for a few Sundays. I didn't go *anywhere* for a few weeks.

****

James's father owned Evans' Cleaners and they were members of some foreign religion, the Nazarenes. I didn't know who the Nazarenes were, but it sounded like tambourines, so I felt that what they did was something like the gypsies because they played tambourines too—so they were gypsy types.

One day, I asked James about his tambourine. His blank stare indicated that he didn't want to reveal the whereabouts of his tambourine. It must have been a religious secret. But that was OK. He could hide his tambourine if he wanted to. He must have had his own religious reasons for hiding it. But I was his friend. His good friend.

One Saturday, James came by to show me his new cap gun, from Kresses. It shined like a dollar and was loud. It was the first time I had ever seen such a toy before. The cap gun was truly realistic. You put these little pieces of paper in a slot, pulled the trigger and *POW*! I had to have one.

James came by to ask if I could do down to Walter's Drug Store. The circus was in town and the clowns and animals were to assemble in front of the drug store. Mother wouldn't let me go. We were supposed to go to Bull Lake for a picnic. I created a total scream hemorrhage but she said a firm *no*. I did evoke from her a promise that I could have a cap gun like James's.

We went to the picnic and had a wonderful afternoon with Onion Robinson, Babe Hammons, and several others. When we came back home, Valtie Hudson was sitting on our front porch. She called Dad and Mother aside and whispered something to them. They came straight to me and said, "Son, we're going to Lubbock to get you a cap pistol."

It never occurred to me that they had cap guns at Kresses. Besides, a trip to Lubbock was a trip to heaven to a small, bored boy. When we got back from the big city, there was a sack inside the screen door. Mother opened it. It was a cap pistol.

The note read: "James would have wanted J. C. to have this." It was signed simply, "Evans."

Dad's face tightened into total grimness. "Let's go around to the back porch." The front porch was for fun; the back porch was for punishment or serious "man" talk. This one was not for a dad-to-son talk. It was a situation that called for a man-to-man.

As we sat down, I looked over the backyard. From there, Mother threw the dish water. She washed with homemade lye soap and threw it in the same spot. No grass grew there, no dog would lie there; no bug could survive passage across the lye-soaked area.

Dad cleared his throat. . . . he cleared it again. . . . "Son, James Evans was killed today. He was popping his cap gun in a leopard's face, and it reached out and tore off the back of his head. Mr. Treadway tried to pull him loose but the leopard bit him bad. That is what Valtie Hudson told us, and that is why we went to Lubbock, so things could settle down."

I didn't really hear anything Dad said. I only heard that James was dead. I threw James's cap gun on the ground and ran out to the barn.

I stayed there until Mother came and got me.

"First Robert . . . then James. I don't like God at all."

By now, the sobs were tearing me apart. Mother rocked me in the rocker and sang to me. It was as though I wanted to be an innocent baby again; but somehow I felt guilty, dirty all over. Sleep finally came. Mother's arms felt good.

Dad sat out on the porch, smoking his pipe and looking at the bright moon reflecting its liquid silver down on the open plains in front of our house.

ELEVEN

Places

God chooses the oddest places to change the world.

TEARDROPS ON HIS BOOTS

John Steinbeck wrote his last book, *Travels with Charley*, about traveling around the country in a small motor home with his dog, Charley. Steinbeck had cancer, wanted to be out of everyone else's hair, tough out the sickness, and die and be a riddance.

He tells of arriving at the continental divide. There was a small hump in the highway, with signs by the side of the road, indicating the place and its significance. He and Charlie got out of the motor home, and Steinbeck straddled the divide, putting one foot on one side, and the other foot on the other side.

He thought upon the fact that if a teardrop fell from his cheeks onto his left shoe, dripping off into the ground, it would ultimately end up in the Pacific Ocean. . . . And if a teardrop fell on his right shoe, dripping off into the ground, it would ultimately end up in the Atlantic Ocean.

The thought staggered him, this dying man, seeking the ultimate meaning of life. He shook his head, and said, "This is too great a fact for such an insignificant place as this."

Great facts appear in insignificant places.

THE LORRAINE HOTEL

As one of Martin Luther King's followers stood by, watching him die, he said, "What a . . . place to die—a cheap motel like the Lorraine!"

Great events occur in insignificant places.

DEALEY PLAZA, DALLAS

I stood on the hot street of the Dealey Plaza in Dallas. The steam seemed to pour out of the hot concrete from the pavement. I thought, "A president of the United States died right at this spot."

At that moment, a little cur dog furtively dashed across the street . . . a quite old car, with a mischievous muffler, belched unwelcome black smoke into my nostrils.

Same thought.

"What a poor choice of a place for the very destiny of a nation to hinge—what a dumb place for a president to die!"

Great events occur in insignificant places.

SMELLING JERUSALEM

Have you ever *smelled* Jerusalem? Sometimes it reeks.

Have you ever listened to Jerusalem? Nine of every ten words spoken are to sell you something, not worth 10 percent of what it costs. And if you do not buy, you are subjected to a kind of scorn that you can feel right down to your heels.

Have you ever touched Jerusalem? It is mostly limestone, the sort that comes off on your clothes like chalk. If you do not feel of Jerusalem, it will feel of you. Two months after the trip, you will swear it is still in your hair and on your clothing.

Have you ever bought anything in Jerusalem? I purchased a wood carving of a Shepherd bringing the lost sheep home. By the time I was back in the USA, the Shepherd's feet had broken off. It was cracked when it was sold.

THE BIRTHPLACE OF JESUS

That's Jerusalem for you!

A caretaker turning the lights out on you, while you are reverently looking at the birthplace of our Lord—because we didn't tip him enough. . . . Being shown *two* authenticated sites where Jesus was beaten, each site with a very prominent offering box. . . . Being sold cheap quality film to photograph Lazarus's tomb. . . . Being badgered to photograph a man and his donkey at the Ascension site on Olivet.

You find yourself asking, "Is there no way to sophisticate the reality from the midway of this carnival?"

TOMMY TIDWELL'S RAG-BAG

Change his attire and the priest rattling his offering plate is Joe Flaherty, working the Crazy House on the big midway of Tommy Tidwell's rag-bag carnival in 1932 in Muleshoe, Texas.

In sifting through these soul traps, I continued looking for that something that made those early, primitive believers radiate so irresistibly. What made them sing through the persecutions, laugh at months of languishing in a damp, dark, rat-infested, prison cell, and giggle just outside of death's door?

I heard that a Scottish pastor-friend of mine once shouted from the dirty streets of Nazareth, "Did my Lord Jesus come from this filthy place?" My feelings were like his . . . until an old minister laid his experience on my exasperation and said, "No, Jess, your Lord didn't come *from* this place. He only came *through* this place."

And while He was sojourning, some few earthlings met Him, fell in love with Him, and caught the *glow*. And when He left, they couldn't forget; they were seized with a desperate nostalgia to be with Him again. Then they remembered His words, freighted with eternity and the bright shimmering of glorious predawn, resurrection light: "I go to prepare a place for you."

No more of this reeking atmosphere, or cracked wooden shepherds, or dusty limestone, or caretakers turning off lights, or contradictory authentications, or blurred film. "I go to prepare a place for you."

Jerusalem was, and is, a place of slain egos. Its wars have been struggles over holy things and holy places. "If you take them away from me, I have no *thou place*."

But the new message is that holy places are not where Jesus *was*, but where He *is*. To all people looking for a place, be reminded that you have, in Christ, an eternal *thou place* . . . and heaven is *that place*! There is a place for you.

"If I go, I will come again, and receive you unto myself."

Everyone has a B.C. story and an A.D. story. This is my *Anno Domini* story.

I shall go to Him through death, or He will come to me "when it all falls down."

So, who cares what happens to us. Cancer? The joy *then* and *there* will overbalance the pain *now* and *here*. Broke? Things in the *ultimate thou place* will be so valuable that they will use gold to pave the streets.

So, while I sweat, weep, and emote *here*, I keep looking up because He might have chosen this day to be the day He chooses. . . . He might have left heaven only this morning en route to pick me up and take me to my permanent *thou place*!

That where I am, there you shall be also. Heaven's joy is not the big houses we get for being very, very good—making heaven that great big Palm Beach in the Sky. It is a place where every tree bears all the fruit you want—that great big Rio Grande Valley up yonder.

No.

The big story about heaven is that the frustrated shall be with the fulfilled *thou*. In the *thou* is fellowship. In the *thou* is life. In the *thou* is peace. In the Thou is enough.

El Shaddai: the God who is enough.

Jehovah Jireh: the God who supplies our needs. *Elohim:* the God of power.

In Jesus dwells the fullness of the Godhead (the Enough, the Supplier, the Power) bodily. And, to think, you shall be like Him: You shall have enough; you shall be supplied; you shall have sufficient motivating power!

No wonder that those formerly frustrated, shrivel self-imaged disciples were so aflame. They didn't require special training courses in witnessing. It would have taken training discipline and heavy restraints to keep them from witnessing. They weren't like modern Christians, always searching; they had found . . . and were running through the streets shouting to friend and foe alike: Not, "Where is it?" but "Eureka!"

They didn't wring their hands. They rang the Liberty Bell. They exchanged their hangups for hallelujahs! The Cross is God's game plan for the universe. Christ is in everything: life! nature! and time!

TWELVE

My Most Incredible Story

What do you do when you are invited to a thousand-dollar-a-plate dinner—gratis? You go, dummy. Right?

So as I sat at this plate of really average food. No silver trays or silk napkins. No Julia Childs's cooking. Just food. Average, plain ordinary food. Truthfully, I cannot remember the occasion.

I do remember that it was at the Breakers in Palm Beach, that some super dignitaries were there, just who I don't recall. But I do remember two things—vividly.

My weird mind concentrated on the *peas*. At one thousand bucks a plate, how much would each pea cost? Let's see, there are forty peas on the plate. That comes to about twenty-five bucks per pea. Einstein was never more analytical.

When you are from Muleshoe, Texas, at a dinner like this, you get analytical, I can promise you that. But the per-pea-price-per-plate (try saying that ten times real fast) was not the most memorable feature of that dinner.

It was my conversation with a good friend named Bev Smith, an elderly automobile magnet from the old "sooth" (his word for *south*).

"I know you love stories, Jess, and I want to affirm that every word of what I am about to tell you is true."

It was a jaw dropper, almost unbelievable; but my verification indicates the absolute truthfulness of it.

During the War Between the States (southern for the Civil War) Bev's family lived in St. Petersburg, Virginia, on the St. Johns River, in an old antebellum and stately house, complete with the Greek pillars, filigreed, large entry doors, and the traditional white front porch surrounding the house. It was out of the path of tears, Sherman's troop movements, therefore harm's way.

Bev was from a large family, a matriarchally dominated, yet with love, home. One of Bev's uncles was a captain in the Confederate Cavalry, who deported himself nobly in battle, demonstrating exceeding heroism, for which he was awarded the Confederate Cross.

Bev's mother was supremely proud of her brother's accomplishments, inordinately so. So much, that every year, she brought out the cross and spoke of his heroism, showing the cross to the family and admonishing them to never give up on southern culture, southern ideals, and southern ways.

One year, she was regaling them with the stories of valor, complete with descriptions of battle. "The Yankees came over this hill, southern troops were deployed to surround them, and destroy their firepower, your brave uncle . . ."

The wonder and glory of it electrified little five-year-old Bev, until he blurted out, "Oh, Mother, may I please wear the cross! Just for an hour. I will be careful with it." She smiled and placed the ribbon and the cross around Bev's neck.

Bev was elated, and charged out of the room to play war with his brothers. He completely lost himself in the emotion of it, running down by the river, around the house, hiding from the Yankee, played by his reluctant brother.

An hour went by like the blink of an eye, as Bev dodged and danced, swirled and whirled, imitating the neighing of dying horses, looking wall-eyed as they fell, covered with sweat, and red-pitted nostrils gasping for air as they went down for the last time. Oh, it was a glorious victory, as Captain Bev stood, flushed and panting from an hour of childhood romp.

As he was savoring the "victory," he reached to feel the Confederate Cross. It was gone! Bev searched everywhere before he repentantly told his mother that it was missing. No one can imagine how desperately they looked, all the children, all the family, the help, just about everyone ransacked the area. It was not to be found.

They all surmised that it had been lost in the river. Bev had run down by the banks during the imagined fracas. That was probably it. God knows where it lay, deep in the mudbank, or washed far down the river.

No one could describe the depth of Bev's pain at the thought of losing the heirloom of all family heirlooms, the great Confederate Cross!

Every year after that, when Mother told her stories about the Captain, she would dramatize the heroics of the great and noble uncle, and how General Lee honored him by placing around his neck the Confederate Cross, *which Bev lost after promising to guard it carefully.*

At this point each year, she would burst into tears, and one time, she ran out of the room, not able to restrain herself, screaming, "Oh, Bev, how could you?" This was designed to greatly enhance Bev's self-image up about knee-high to a boll weevil.

The years went by. Mother died; and, almost to her last day, reminded Bev of his error. She did utter forgiveness, but even then with a hint of a grudge.

Bev was now a mature man, successful, and a good Christian. He and his brother, Bill, were assigned the task of breaking up the old household, distributing the furniture, selling what nobody wanted.

It was all settled and done. Bev and Bill walked around the old place, laughed at the antics of all the kids, remembered their long-dead father and now, mother. They sat down in the large, empty living room, their voices echoing in the huge space for just one last memory.

"What do you remember most about Momma, Bill?"

"I remember her roses. She won several awards at the county fair with those giant, big-as-your-head roses. Just look out in the front yard. They are still great looking."

Then Bill seemed to light up. "I'm going to dig up one of them and plant it in my garden at home."

"Great idea, Bill. I want to do that too."

So each one dug up a small rose bush, put it in a can, and carried it home. Bev planted his in the flower garden in his large back yard. It flourished, and each spring presented a love offering in memory of his mother.

A year later, Bev was faced with some pretty heavy stuff, and he became quite depressed. He always worked in his garden to relieve any tension he was feeling.

He wanted, desperately, to please his mother, during his childhood; and many times he would talk with her about his little hurts, put his head in her lap, and she would rub his head until he would fall asleep. Then she would carry him to his room, and later he would waken in his own bed, under his own covers.

That was the best sleep he ever experienced. "Mama sleep," he called it. Now, sitting in his garden, successful tycoon Bev Smith needed his mother's touch. "Mama, I need some brow stroking. I am faced with a dozen problems I can't solve. Help me, please."

He picked up his little garden spade, and starting digging around his mother's rose. It struck something.

Bev started digging around the roots of the rosebush. And there, clutched in the roots, was *the great Confederate Cross!*

Bev looked at me, tears brimming in his eyes, and said something I shall never forget. "Many people get away from God, *only to rediscover the Cross, held solidly in the roots of his mother's love.*"

THIRTEEN

Mother's Ph.D.

I recall the day I left for college. Mother had packed everything, more than I would ever need. I could have blessed the Salvation Army with a gift of half of what she crammed in those two old bags.

Dad didn't say much. He never did; but that day, he was unusually quiet. For a quiet man to cause those around him to think that he is *unusually* quiet is a quiet you can hear, a sub river flowing below the quiet. You feel the tremors coming from the quiet.

"Son," he finally spoke, "I was able to get only a third grade education. It has crippled me all my life. I had to learn grammar, reading, and figuring the hard way, by listening to smart people talk, and copying them. I was forty years old before I learned to spell. (The truth is, he never did learn to spell with *exactness*—but he *stabbed* at it, and came close to exactness every fourth or fifth word. That was exact enough for him.)

"As you go to college, learn something, but don't get so educated that you look down on common people like Mother and me. When you get educated *up* to where you are comfortable with just folks, then you have become pretty smart; good, plain, God-fearing people will trust you—and that will make you a success. Talk from what you know, not in order to make people think you know more than you know. Common people can smell out a smart-aleck. I have been sick all my life, and—hurting as I was—I don't need some smart-aleck to make me feel worse, or inferior.

"Just remember, everybody, *everybody*, from the president on down to the likes of me, is hurting. You'll always have a job if you can take away soul hurting, and body-and-mind hurting. People will pay big money to buy some of that.

"Learning is making stupidity retreat. God knows, there is a lot of stupidity around. Kill off as much of it as you can, and remember, *God has not called us to see through each other; but he has called us to see each other through.* He is going to ask you: 'How many people did you see through?' I'll bound you (Dad's word for *bet*) that just after He checks you out about how you feel about Jesus, that's what He's goin' to ask you."

Then, I saw my father do something I had never seen him do before. He *cried.*

That did it for Mother. She had a Ph.D. in crying, so she broke up like a hard winter. Vesuvius could not have done it better.

The bus driver, feeling the sensitivity of the moment, said gently, "Time to go, folks."

Mother kissed and cried, and cried and kissed.

Dad, who had just delivered the longest and best speech of his life, said still more: "Here's twenty dollars that Mother and I have saved to help you. Get them to give you every help they can, and send us the bill for the rest. We'll make do somehow. Do the best you can, Son. That's all a mule can do."

As the bus pulled out from the service station, which was the terminal in our small town, I waved good-bye to the two dearest things that had happened to me in *all* my seventeen years. I watched them as long as I could see them.

Mother, who had dressed up as if it were Sunday to see me off, and Dad, shoulders slightly drooped from giving in to an almost habitual chest pain, just standing there, watching the only son they had go away to a college—Baylor University— that sounded to them like the moon.

Since then, I have earned some degrees, built some churches, founded Palm Beach Atlantic College, taught at the largest seminary in the world, Southwestern Baptist Theological Seminary, and preached around the globe. All of that based on a shove given me by a little talk by a simple, loving man who had saved up twenty dollars to get me going.

Every week, I received two dollars spending money, which always came a little late because the folks at the Baylor post office had trouble reading Dad's handwriting.

Jarrel McCracken, the founder of Word, Inc., reminded me of a letter Dad sent to me. It read: "To Jess Moody, Best dam preecher in the u.s.of A (bettr bee!)" That is exactly how it read!

When I flunked Greek, Dad wrote, "Don't wory about them greeks. Ther all ded, anyhow. You only hav to tawk to Americans." To Dad, going to Houston was foreign missions.

I have learned some few things in life; but I never had a professor who said anything better than Dad's quotes to me:

God hasn't called you to see through people. God has called you to see people through.

When you get educated up to where you are comfortable with just folks, then you have become pretty smart; good, plain God-fearing people will trust you.

Common people can smell out a smart-aleck. I have been sick all my life, and—hurting as I was—I don't need some smart-aleck to make me feel worse, or inferior.

Just remember, everybody, everybody, from the president on down to the likes of me, is hurting. You'll always have a job, if you can take away soul hurting, and body-and-mind hurting. People will pay big money to buy some of that.

Learning is making stupidity retreat. God knows, there is a lot of stupidity around. Kill off as much of it as you can.

Do the best you can, Son. That's all a mule can do.

Recently, I presided at my uncle Pete's funeral in San Angelo, Texas. He was Dad's twin brother. Dad died in 1964, at sixty-one. Pete died in 1997, at ninety-four.

Dad married one time, to Connie. Pete married eight times. I asked Pete why he married so many times.

"I was tradin' up."

I've often wondered about the ancient question: "When he gets to heaven, who's husband shall he be?"

I told his "trading up" quote at Pete's funeral. It scandalized none of the family. They just chuckled.

After Pete's funeral, I stood over Dad and Mother's two little slabs, flat against the earth. I thought of that day at the bus station, with Mother kissing me and crying, and crying and kissing me. And I thought of Dad.

I said, "Thanks, Horace Frazier Moody, for the best advice a man could ever receive. At seventy-two, I hope I've done about all a mule can do."

As I walked from his grave to the car, I stopped, turned around, and said, "And thanks for the twenty bucks."

FOURTEEN

Cap'n Rudy

It had been one of those "Will I ever make it till the end of the week?" days.

Overload from 5:00 A.M.

It had leaked out from that mighty gossip, Chief Word-of-Mouth, that I was one of those 4:00 A.M. people, and every insomniac in town felt led to call.

Coupled with that, I was smack-dab in the middle of the male midlife crisis. They call it *menopause* when it is a woman. I call it *metapause* when it is a man. The man will get either another woman or some weird, out-of-character hobby.

I had been one of those tippy-toe-and-talk-nice preachers, and there was this roaring call of the wild raging in my breast and my loins . . . and you can't tell people how you feel or you'll be defrocked by sunset if you do.

Since Doris was more than I could handle, I opted for two paramours: my BMW motorcycle and a sailboat named "Sailbad the Sinner," a forty-footer made by Nathaniel

Herreshoff for Commodore Vanderbilt in 1905. Herreshoff was commissioned to make eighteen of the most sleek, low-slung racing vessels. Originally called the *Nautilus,* she was launched at New York Yacht Club in May of '05.

Every weekend from 1905 through 1913, these beautiful paramours for other "metapausers" of other days slid magnificently through the waters around the New York Yacht Club, of which commodore Vanderbilt was the commodore who out-commodored all other commodores of that era. That was a lot of commodoring, believe me.

When I met the *Nautilus,* it was love at first sight. She was preening in the morning sun up near the Jupiter Lighthouse.

When a man is bitten by the metapause bug, there is very little you can do with him except let him run—especially if he decides that the paramours will be motorcycles and boats. If that is the way it plays out, a wife should take him to the bank and *help* him withdraw the money to buy it.

That's cheaper than a divorce—and a great contributor to family values. My advice to the wife is that she go to the library and study boats until she smells like the sea wind coming over the fresh morning beach. He will literally *adore* her for it.

On this particular morning, I mounted my "Beemer" (my BMW 750 motorcycle, to be exact), and headed up Jupiter way, thinking that my movie actor friend might be available to have breakfast at Hojo's in Juno.

We did that, and I headed back to where *Sailbad* was moored, at the Eighth Street Marina. The marina was small, but sort of proud because she housed some pretty impressive vessels in the winters. One of them was the *Marlin*, President Kennedy's lovely old girl, built in the twenties or early thirties, still beautiful, forever so, like Loretta Young.

Sailbad could hold her own, but everyone at the dock knew that at seventy-plus years, she wasn't in the same class as these formidable ladies, owned by the people with the *big bucks.*

Sailbad was proud. She kept her mast held high and didn't get vericose rudder. She was the *Padre's* boat, so they tolerated her presence, with very little condescension. In fact, I felt that they kind of liked having this old museum piece around. They were also kind to *Pastor El Cheapo* whenever I strolled around, as though I belonged there.

That morning, I started cleaning up the old girl. She sang her *mast-song* to me as I was rolling up her lines, tightening up the rigging, daubing a bit of epoxy, and touching up her decking with a little mahogany varnish.

A voice behind me clipped out in Bostonese, "Mo'nin'!"

I didn't need to turn about. Without looking up, I chuckled back, "Morning, Cap'n Rudy!"

He was a leather face from Dedham, Massachusetts, who wore his pants on legs bowed by nearly eighty years, mostly at sea. He was like the bowlegged man of whom Shakespeare spoke, "Ho, what manner of men are these, who wear their trousers on parentheses!"

I knew what he wanted. "There's some fresh-brewed coffee from fresh-ground beans. The pot is singing *Padreee, come aboard!*"

It was a real kick-in-the-pants to sit aboard his sleek, multi-million-dollar yacht, owned by the Brown Shoe Company.

Rudy loved the phrase "unleaded" as I described my desire for no decaf. It meant that I was aboard, and I listened to Rudy's tales from the sea. He could weave a wondrous litany of unusual sea sagas.

He asked, "How's it faring?"

"Faring only fair," I said.

"What's the rub?" he asked.

Well, part of it was a bit humorous. There were two guys who worked at the dock. One was Jack and the other, John. Word came that Jack had died, and I was to preach the funeral. I am not great with names and faces; and I had the two of them mixed up, in my mind. It was a closed-casket funeral, so I thought I had buried the one who was named Jack.

"Rudy, imagine my feelings this morning when the one I thought was Jack, whom I had just buried the week before, came walking up to me."

"Hi, Reverend!" he said.

"You can't be here. I buried you last week!"

"I don't think so. I would have remembered an incident like *that!*"

I thought John was Jack and Jack was John. Rudy cackled out laughter from his happy face and smiling eyes. From then on, we called him "Lazarus"—back from the dead.

After we settled down and warmed ourselves with Rudy's incomparable coffee, I returned to my "only fair" routine.

Palm Beach Atlantic College, where I was serving as president, was struggling financially. . . . My church was an endless round of activity, with more than a hundred programs of all types going on. . . . I was chaplain of the PGA, and some of the pros were at each other's throats until I thought they were going to kill each other. . . . Divorces were pouring in on me, with all the refereeing you must do with that. . . . One of my staff members was caught in a moral scandal. I was trying to save as much benefit out of it as I could. . . . There was much more, so I was dancing to the rhythm of the bots and the blues.

"I have a story for you that will just hit the spot," Rudy said. Somehow, I knew this was coming.

I was a thousand miles off the African Coast in a little freighter, heading for Newport News. She was quite old, metal-fatigued, and rivet-rusted. Suddenly, a horrendous storm hit with frightening fierceness. I had had a "red sea at dawning," and the sailor had not taken warning.

The swells were huge, and torrents of water nearly broached us several times. The crew—I included—could not measure the terror we felt. After a day and a night of it, I began to hear the rivets pop. *PING! POW!* A rivet would pop every few minutes. Every time a rivet would pop, the vessel grew weaker . . . and my hope factor plummeted. The thought occurred to me, *This seems a good time to pray.*

Seamanship I knew. In normal times, handling the Dedham Dasher had been nothing. I was pretty weak on prayer, though. The thought then struck me: Bobby, our mech, had just become religious; but he was below deck, green with sickness. I lashed the wheel, dashed down to his bunk. There he lay, as I said, pea-green sick.

"Where's that Gideeean Bible you've been reading?"

"You mean the Gideon Bible—it's in my duffel bag."

I scrambled through his stuff until I found the Bible. A stupid thought came to my mind as I saw the green Gideon Bible. Bobby and the Bible were the same color.

I scurried back up topside, took over the helm, and began looking for something I could use. I started at the beginning, about Adam and Eve, even Noah and the Ark, but nothing seemed to help. I looked in the back of the Bible, where there were Gideon helps. I found the story of Jesus calming the sea. *That's it,* I thought! The rain was pouring in my face. I put my finger on the passage, and screamed into the wind: "OK, God, DO IT!"

The wind seemed to increase. I heard another distant *PING! POW!* I screwed up my courage—surmising that faith was courage turned skyward—and yelled again: "If You don't mind, Lord, I would appreciate it if You hurry it up a bit. This tub has just so many rivets in it."

Another responded: *PING! POW!*

I felt complete desperation, looked up in the rain, and yelled at top voice, "OK, God, storm or no storm, I BELIEEEEVE!"

The storm and the pinging and powing lasted two more days. The *Dedham Dasher* held together, and we limped, tired and wounded, into the Miami port a few days later.

I learned to trust the slowness and the sureness of God—in spite of the fears and the PING, POWS!

FIFTEEN

The Seaman's Prayer

O God . . .
Thy sea is so great and my boat is so small . . .
Fill my sails with the winds of the Spirit.
Keep my eyes ever upon the compass of Thy Word . . .
. . . And let me survey the horizon in search of undiscovered Islands of Wonder . . .
. . . And at the end of my journey, please lead me into the quiet Harbor of the Haven of Rest,
To sail the wild seas no more.
The tempest may sweep o'er the wild, stormy deep . . .
But in Jesus, I am safe, forevermore!
In the Name of Christ, my Pilot, I pray.
AMEN.

SIXTEEN

Talitha Cumi!

Carl and Caroline Graves had four children—three, healthy. At the hospital the fourth lay in a coma for four months. Her name: Tina—they called her Tinker.

Carl and Caroline made a decision about Christmas. Caroline would stay home, putting together a slender Christmas for the other children. Neighbors from the church had made a little tree, complete with ornaments. There was practically no food in the refrigerator.

Carl stayed at the hospital with Tinker.

Caroline wakened the children, and they sat around the tree wide-eyed, but knowing it would be a limited Christmas. They stoically pretended to be anxious about what Santa had brought them.

They lived outside of town in a small home, so when Caroline heard a car door slam, she went to the window to look out. It was the pastor, Reverend Lynch, Carl, and some other person still in the car.

Seeing the pastor with Carl made Caroline fear the worst. "Oh, dear God, not on Christmas morning! Not on Christmas morning!" Fear clutched her throat. Anxiety raged. She told the children to stay in by the tree. She would go to the door.

When she opened the door, there stood Carl. "I had to come home Christmas morning to be with my family; and I have a Christmas present for you."

Pastor Lynch handed a bundle to Carl. He opened a blanket, uncovering Tinker! Weak, wan, sickly, but with her eyes open!

"Hi, Mommie!"

A riot of praise broke out in the room! The children came running, singing, and dancing. Caroline held little Tinker in her arms, and baptized the baby with her tears.

Dr. Ousler, the other member of the foursome, said, "I came just to make sure everything was all right. Tinker will make it, now . . ." the doctor started weeping ". . . now that she's home!"

After they all settled down to mild uproar, Carl told what had happened. "Early this morning, around 6:00 A.M., I leaned over Tinker and said 'Merry Christmas, Tinker.' I told the Christmas story and sang old Christmas songs. Then, I prayed, 'Dear God, You gave Tinker to us. It is Christmas morning. If You want to take her home, we give her as a gift to You.'

"I didn't hear voices from God; but I heard with my heart the Lord clearly say, 'No, I give her to you. *You* take her home.'

"I looked at Tinker. Her eyes fluttered. She looked at me and said, 'Hi, Daddy!' She is very weak. We can open the gifts, but the doctor and I have to take her back. You did get Tinker a gift, didn't you?"

"Of course!" Caroline replied. "And I got one for you, Carl. I made it myself."

Ginger, the oldest daughter, opened Tinker's present. It was a little doll Tinker had wanted, and Caroline had made some little dresses for it. Tinker smiled and snuggled the little doll up close to her little heart.

"This is for you, Carl," Caroline said, handing him a small package. "It was something I made for us."

The gift was a framed motto. It read, *"Talitha cumi."*

When Jairus's daughter died, Jesus came to his house, held the little girl's hand, and said, *"Talitha cumi."* It means "Little lamb, arise."[1]

---

1. Based on a story presented by Beverly LaHaye, radio program, Christmas Eve, 1996.

SEVENTEEN

Little Boy Dreams

Every child needs a secret place of his own. I had one, actually two, "thou places" of my own. One was in my sailboat, "Sailbad the Sinner."

I remember that Pat, our son, was at the helm, and some other crewmates were on deck, telling jokes and laughing. I was below, in my bunk—my *thou place*—just meditating, and thinking, and praying. We were about twenty miles out, heading from West Palm Beach to Lucaya in the Bahamas.

My dream machine was red hot. I was so inspired that I believe I could have written another *Messiah* right then and there. The writing juices were flowing! Here I was, a man, a pastor, at sixty years of age . . . but I wasn't sixty. I was seven, lying on the warm rug on a chilly night, in front of our fireplace in our little house on the prairie, in Littlefield, Texas. It was 1932.

My parents had left to do some shopping. Our home was mine, mine alone, the palace of boyhood dreams; through my mind soldiers marched, and I was astride Trixie, my horse, my good friend. I was riding into battle against the deadly Hun . . . and the hum of a shell passing near my head disturbed me not in the least.

I had no time for shot and shell; I was riveted—completely single minded—upon the mission of rescuing John Henry and Babe Hammons, my schoolmates, from the clutches of the grim enemy.

For some reason, the German troops must have thought that I was one of them. They didn't notice me. I leapt from Trixie, quickly into the back of the tent where they were being held.

With my bowie knife my folks had given me for Christmas, I cut open the back of the tent, went in, cut loose Babe and John Henry. I warned them that they must be very quiet. I put them on Trixie, then hit her on the rump. She sped off in the inky darkness, carrying my two grateful friends, who waved their "Godspeed" to me. Inspiration was on their faces as they thought of my incredible bravery.

My work was cut out for me. I had to negotiate those enemy lines. A rifle could crack in the night, and I would be a candidate for Flander's Field, where poppies grow, and the crosses stand, row on row. But no, I had made it past the long hedgerow. They hadn't seen me . . . yet.

I was working my way back to the safety of our warm campfire by the river, far behind the enemy lines. I wondered and prayed that John Henry and Babe would make it to the other side. . . .

Twelve years later in the real world, they each made it to the warm fire of our friendly camp by the river of life, dying in another war far, far away. . . . But now, I was running full blast in the darkness. The enemy had spotted me. The whiz and whine of shells passing me, whizzing and whining for my blood. I heard their hounds, yelping for my track. I saw the friendly camp across the river. I leaped into the river and swam as hard as my seven-year-old body would allow me. . . . The enemy was about to catch me! Would they?

I saw Babe and John Henry on the other shore, cheering for me. I had almost made it. Would I? Could I? Just then, I heard a familiar sound.

"Hi, Hon! Were we gone too long?" It was Mom, with her arm filled with groceries . . . and Dad, right behind her. . . .

Then, I heard another sound. It was Patrick, who had interrupted the interruption by my parents of my great, heroic run-for-life clear up to the warm campsite. "Come on up, Dad, you're missing the most beautiful night of your dreams."

Ah! The night of my dreams. "Coming up, Son."

I was as angry as hops at both my parents and my son, who had interrupted the interruption of my great dream, in the dream factory of my bunk down below.

Every child simply must have such an enchanting, secret place where pictures dance through the mind like sugar plum fairies . . . and fancy pirouettes . . . and every flower has a face, and every act is punctuated by adjectival alacrity. Children are dream factories, where future destinies are born.

I recall an afternoon in Littlefield, Texas, a long, long time ago. The Hammons brothers, the Dunagin, Renfro, Chapman boys were all at our house, where the Wildcat Bowl was played every day. Our minds saw one hundred thousand people surrounding the large field next to our house.

It was here that we all played our hearts out every day that summer. Our uniforms were shiny bright reds, blues, hues of green, gold orange, white, and purple. We played Notre Dame, Michigan, the University of Texas, and the Aggies . . . all in our dreams . . . all in our dreams.

One day, immediately after a glorious victory over Michigan, we were all lying in that cocoon of wonder where every child lives from time to time. I am not at all certain that I can verbalize my feelings as I lay there with that warm-cool fall breeze kissing my cheeks.

Valhalla!

For reasons I cannot explain, a thick cloud of wonder hovered over me. The good fairy who gives dreams, leaned over me and gently touched my head with her soft hand. My mind started spinning . . . the flowered fields mixed their colors into a rainbow whip, which covered me from head to toe.

I was *allliivvee*—alive—with the great idea machine whipping up in my spirit. I suddenly leapt up and ran into our barn, and began pulling out huge cardboard boxes that Dad had stored something in; but they were now empty and tempting the rainbow mind of a small boy.

One box became headquarters, the main office. Another box was the dining hall. Still another was the dormitory. This was "*Moody Military Academy.*" I was the Captain. I shared my dream of the founding of a school that was different, better, than any school that had ever been. A military school of the first order!

I shared my dream with the other boys. Not one of them protested. Each and all were faculty, students . . . and we were a part of something wonderfully impossible to bring about, bigger than we could imagine.

Some of the boys were dressed in imaginary uniforms—more glorious than anything the academies could dream up. Bands were playing. Proud parents were everywhere, beaming at our greatness. All the girls in school were in the giant stadium, cheering for us as we marched in elegant perfection while the royal band, who sailed here—sent by King George—to play for our school. Bettye Ruth Walters, Helen Heathman, Connie Hopping, and scores of other adoring schoolmates and teachers and principals, and superintendents—and even the janitor—cheered and cheered and cheered for *us*.

The Royal Band was directed by Morgan Layfield, our local bandmaster, who was chosen as the best in the world by fifteen kings and presidents who came to Washington, D.C., to make the choice. All of this magnificence parading in and around the campus of cardboard boxes plus a boy's imagination. That was 1938.

In 1963, I was lying in my bed in predawn sleep skimming, when suddenly a flash of light—from God, I believe—hammered into my brain. I sat bolt upright in bed, wakening my Doris. "I am called to found a college, different from any other. One such as a man dared not dream possible, with a different stance, a different philosophy than any school ever born." We had nothing but old buildings, only slightly better than cardboard boxes. Cardboard boxes—and a dream.

Today, it is a magnificent college, facing the shimmering waters of Palm Beach. Palm Beach Atlantic College stands today, because my parents never stifled my little-boy dreams.

Jesus turned mere water into vivacious wine. Actually, the pure water saw the perfect face of Christ—and blushed into the redness of the best wine.

He also changed cardboard boxes into a towering college, where thousands of young people have been prepared to march into the shimmering tomorrows!

Who said a child's faith was impractical. Faith is the first principle of practical engineering! It is *faithineering!*

EIGHTEEN

The Clockmaker and the Wise Old Hermit

Mr. Stanley was the signalman at the giant industrial plant, and he came down the same street on his way to work every day for twenty-five years. As he jaunted along, he passed Mr. Helman's jewelry store at about the same time each morning. There was a giant grandfather's clock just inside the door. The signalman would set his watch each day by the old clock.

At five in the afternoon, Mr. Stanley had the responsibility of blowing the whistle, signaling closing time. After all these many years, Mr. Stanley retired. On his last day of work, he came at his usual time by Mr. Helman's store.

"Helman, this is my last day to come by the store. I'm retiring. It looks like I won't be setting my watch by the old grandfather's clock any more."

Mr. Stanley didn't understand why Mr. Helman burst into laughter.

"Is it *that* funny that I am retiring?"

"No, no," Helman replied. "What *is* funny is that every evening, I set my grandfather's clock by your five o'clock whistle!"

Then, there is the story of the wise old hermit in the high mountains. A new merchant in the valley community had built two sheds to hold firewood for sale in the winter. Since he was new in the area, he had no idea how cold the winter would be. So, he sent his apprentice up the mountains to talk to the wise old hermit, who was very insightful about nature.

He was the wise old hermit in the high mountains, you see.

The apprentice came back all fired up: "Sir, he says this winter will be very, very cold!"

The apprentice reported back "We'd better build another shed, if the winter is to be so cold."

So, they built another shed. After filling up the new shed, the merchant sent the apprentice back up the mountain to the wise old hermit to make sure he was adequately prepared. The apprentice came back down more excited than before. The old hermit had told him that the winter would be worse than he had thought.

So, up went another shed, and it was filled even faster.

This time, the merchant was so impatient that he decided to go up to talk to the old hermit himself.

"Wise old gentleman, tell me—what will the winter be like?"

Without a word, the hermit went to the ledge, looked to the valley for a long, long time. Then, he returned and said, "Coming winter, worst I have ever seen!"

"But how do you know?"

"Easy. Merchant-in-valley gathers so much wood."

No wonder we do not know the times or the seasons. We are getting our information from each other, then echoing it back and forth, and forth and back.

NINETEEN

Burt and "Sailbad the Sinner"

*Dedicated to Burt Reynolds Sr.,
and Fern, whose no-nonsense living
has inspired and taught me lessons
Harvard knows nothing about.*

Burt Reynolds and I have been friends since he and I were young men. He was a hard-charging young actor working on a series called *River Boat*. He hated being on that series because the lead actor had so much control over the show; and he was a little—or a lot—jealous of B. R. He strictly restricted what B. R.'s lines would be.

B. R. had trouble learning his lines because they were so lengthy, like "Yep," "No," and the line that he had the most problem remembering, "Who?"

THE DAY BURT LOST HIS TEMPER

Burt's temper was under control about the situation until the day he went into the producer's office to talk about it.

Every time B. R. started explaining his problem, the phone would ring; and the producer would answer, then take five minutes to get off that call. This went on about six times, and B. R. had had it. He took the phone, ripped it out of the wall, and calmly said, "Now, will you listen—please?"

That was the impulsive, young Burt. He has mellowed out now, as I hope I have.

I was the pastor of the First Baptist Church of West Palm Beach, a hard charger, full of vim, vigor, and vitality—interested in ministerial success. If Baptists had had a pope, that would have been my goal!

Burt's youth was bittersweet—more sweet than bitter; but the bitter was *bitter.* Actually, he was more better than bitter; but the bitter was there nonetheless. It was caused by an accident, which ruined his knees and a promising football career.

Watson P. Duncan III, the drama professor at Palm Beach Junior College, took this brooding young Marlon Brando look-alike and put him in some college plays, where he immediately, after some Duncan polishing, stole the show. He went to Hollywood, landed some parts, finally ending up on *River Boat,* and pulling phones out of walls.

He came to see me about some matter (for the life of me, I can't remember what it was). Out of it came a true friendship that has weathered time for thirty years.

I later married Burt and Loni—but I'm not going to get into *that!*

Ours is that sort of relationship that, when you haven't seen each other for a year, the conversation begins with "Like I was saying, . . ."

PREACHERS AND ACTORS

Burt is quite comfortable to be around, watch, listen to, and talk with. There is not the sense of unease that usually exists when actors meet preachers They both seem to fall into a parrying, thrusting kind of stilted talk. Both sides need to lighten up a little bit—no, a lot!

B. R. and I don't have that, and don't want it. He has that old fashioned masculine integrity. He keeps his word. If he can't, due to circumstances beyond his control, he'll make it right and explain it fully—to your satisfaction.

SAILBAD THE SINNER

We sailed together on my 1905 Herreschof New York '30. She was named *Sailbad the Sinner.* (Isn't that a lovely name for a preacher's boat?)

I remember one day we were about a mile off Palm Beach, plowing southerly. It was a rich day, freighted with good vibes, the fresh mothering of a spring morning.

Sailbad was singing to us, the fingers of the wind were strumming the strings of the rigging with an ageless music that mariners a thousand years ago hummed to.

The briny breezes, the thrilling comfort of the alternating warm-to-chill breathing the breath of ecstasy, the feel of the weal of gratitude for the experience of the day, simply penetrates right through your soul and you, for a fleeting moment, believe you can walk on water!

We each knew what the other was thinking, and nodded agreement that it was a darned fine day. It was so fine that my thoughts turned to Burt's relationship to God.

I don't believe it does a bit of permanent good just to feel good about God, on a "darned fine day."

I believe that through Christ, that kind of morning can get into your soul, and when life's winter gives its worst frost-biting blast, you can still feel the warm chill, smell the briney breezes, and hear the harpsong in the rigging of the soul.

Inside—and permanently.

So, I told him the way I felt, that he really should square himself away with the Lord. And he did what a lot of people do when we edge in, a little too close for the psyche's comfort. He changed the subject.

"What is the name of your dinghy?"

"The little boat that shadows us, like a detective? *Oh, that?*"

Burt howled with that weird laugh that won the gold in the Worldwide Weird Laugh Competition.

"Yeah, what do you call it?"

"Dinghys don't have names" I said.

"Everything deserves a name, especially if it follows as faithfully as that little dinghy has done. And where is the official book that decrees that dinghys don't have names?"

"Well, what shall we call this persistent little friend?"

Quick as a silver, he said, "'Goodness 'n' Mercy,' because it shall follow me all the days of my life!"

The humorous, witty, sometimes spiritual mind showed me why he was so successful in his profession, or whatever profession he might have chosen.

GOD-TALK AGAIN

So, Burt got me off track when I began talking about spiritual things, and like a bullet, I went right back to the God-talk again.

So, I cast my dialogue about faith in a semi-humorous vein, striking the pose and vocal placement like that of a tent evangelist, who punches out a canned, twisted-mouthed carnival pitch, with leather lungs:

"AND NOW—UH—I AM TELLING YOU, BROTHER REYNOLDS—UH—TURN OR BURN—UH—REPENT OR PERISH—UH—EITHER BELIEVE ON CHRIST OR SWIM ASHORE—UH!"

With that, Burt leapt overboard!

I calculated that this wasn't the day for Burt to come to the altar of faith. But, inside, I knew that day would come!

TWENTY

Whatever Happened to Bill Betts?

*Dedicated to Betty Betts Thomas, the Betts children,
and all the Methodist pastors, such as E. Stanley Jones
and all the little-known ones like Bill Betts.*

"If you can get it out of your hand, I'll catch it."

That's what Bill Betts said.

Right there in the huddle, with the rain pouring down in buckets, and the football as slick as goose grease.

I squirted it out of my hand in the direction he was supposed to be. He caught it. Scored the only touchdown in the game. Bill beat 'em all by himself.

That was the way he faced life. If the odds were one thousand to one, he'd find the one. He majored in fun, was the best dancer in town, knew more practical jokes than all of us, and just everybody couldn't take their eyes off him.

Town clown.

But Mr. Respect.

A member of the Filthy Three, made up of Betts, Moody, and Frank Shannon—who is another good story within himself.

But this one is about Bill.

The day Bill told me that God had called him into the ministry, I laughed and braced myself for the punch line. There wasn't one. This was Bill-Betts serious. He never wavered from that day. The cross was before him. The world behind him.

It was Bill Betts who modeled the first consistent Christian before me. It remade my life. I became open to the call. And it came.

Jesus was the Living Water. Bill was the pump.

Years later, when we were both pastors, Bill in Greenville, Texas; and I in West Palm Beach, Florida, I called him, and we kidded a while. Then Bill became deadly serious. "Jess, remember that every time you preach, you must make your pulpit a miniature Calvary, and make every sermon a time and place where you die a little bit."

Two days later, Bill stood up to preach, opened his Bible, and read, "I have been crucified with Christ and I no longer live, but Christ lives in me. The life I live in the body, I live—"

Right there, Bill dropped dead in his pulpit.

Whatever happened to Bill Betts? Was he one minute a living human being? The next, some chemicals lying there, with no more life or meaning than three or four dollars worth of lifeless material? Something that was in the pile of chemicals left, exited. What was it and where did it go?

Whatever happened to the Bill Betts who lived there?

Right here, I must become bitter or better, cynic or sincere. I must have more than a love of happy endings, always wanting everything to end like an old Jimmy Stewart movie, with all the villains quenched, every bill paid, and the whole world cheering the victory.

Or I must resort to that sad image of an older man facing the grim sarcasm of death, and my insides eaten up with the gall of hatred for life, considering Christianity some sort of educated voodooism, a whistling in the dark—with nothing out there but more night.

People search for meaning after death. They cling to their stories of people who died and, a few minutes later, came back to report of the tunnel, the great light, etc. Or they put their hope in some medical journal that a ultra violet lamp encircling the body of a dying person has something go through it at the moment of expiring. What in the heck is that all about?

I don't intend for a moment to be a pencil-pushing prognosticator at this point. But I have held the hands of scores of people as they died. I have witnessed hundreds of death. I am a Bill-Betts-made pastor.

And I demand reality, as he always did. I have come to believe, not by naive rubber-stamping, but by witnessing life and death as a pastor/participant with the event. . . . And I have watched those who placed their bets on the line with Jesus Christ, and those who haven't.

Conclusion?

I am a hands-on, fade-the-shooter, double-the-bet, raise-the-ante Christian, who'll lay it all on the line . . . that Jesus Christ will beat doubt fifty-to-one every time!

I don't believe in luck. I believe in Jesus Christ. Straight out, my belief is that flat-as-flounder, everything the Bible says about life after death is true. I believe also that everything Jesus Christ said about life before death is true. Why should I not believe everything He said about life *after* death? All of life, from here to eternity, is covered by the Bible, which is that sense without which sense all other sense is nonsense.

Life is no crap shoot. I'm no deist either. What good is a God to whom you have no access? If you are going to go the route of hoping that there is life after death, you might as well go bowling. Or punt. I won't punt and give the ball to the devil.

I will tell you flatly that I have walked with Jesus for fifty-nine years—He'll do to ride the River with!

Jesus and the Bible, Coach and Playbook, a winning combo. OK, so what does the Playbook say about the two-minute drill, the last few seconds of the game? Do you want it straight or do you want it tippy-toe-and-talk-nice? I'm too near the Final Gun to waltz.

So, here goes.

The Playbook gives the whole plan for life after death. There are three heavens, according to the Playbook.

1. Clouds (Gen. 1:8–9)
2. Where the stars are (Gen. 1:14–19)
3. This third heaven is where earth-dead believers go (John 14:1–6)

a) It was created before the earth (Job 38:4–7)
b) Why did He make it? God had to build a platform for the performance of praise (Ps. 8:3–8; Col. 1:15–18; and Rev. 4:11)
c) It is a place to use the rewards God gives us (1 Cor. 3:11–14)

That is what the Playbook says.

No stuttering and stammering like some sophomore preacher in college, trying to mouth his class outline on heaven. Clear. And there are a hundred more verses to go with them. Heaven is a place. Not some other dimension. It is big.

It has cities (Heb. 11:10–15; 13:14), thrones (Dan. 7:9–10), mansions (John 14:1–3), books (Luke 10:20), keys (Rev. 9:1), trumpets (Rev. 8:2), food (Rev. 2:7,17), bowls (Rev. 15:7), tables (Luke 22:30), fountains(Rev. 7:17), trees (Rev. 2:7), streets (Rev. 22:1–3), animals (Rev. 19:11), pillars (Job 26:11), mountains (Rev. 14:1), same things as earth (without sin) (Phil. 2:10), unutterable things that people wouldn't believe if they saw them (2 Cor. 12:1–4).

It's all in the Playbook! You want more, Mr. Skeptic? I can give it to you all day long! You stand around, putting ideas in your human mind, a low-power station, representing one-five-billionth of the population of one of the lesser planets in a billion-star galaxy—and dare tell the Creator of that galaxy that your opinion is as good as His!

And that galaxy maker does the most astounding thing ever done for mortal man: He lets His Son become one of those lesser planet people, and those lesser planet-ers, seeing His deity rebuke their human sinfulness, and they killed Him!

That great Creator allowed that death of His perfect Son to count for the righteousness for those lesser planet inhabitants. Man, that's love that's out of this world!

Now, back from the interstellar spaces, to the original question: Whatever happened to Bill Betts?

I have already covered some of it; but there is more. The Playbook gives us monster megabytes of information, so let's focus on just a little of it.

Bill went to heaven, which is a real place for real people—not an accumulation of clouds, where a musician's union of harp players plunk away forever. That would be my definition of a mental institution or hell! Nor are its inhabitants some formless protoplasm, or the life idea, commingled with all other life ideals into a gob, a kind of witless nirvana.

Heaven is a real place, where redeemed people live productive lives unimpeded by sin and aging, a place of great fun and excitement, and where everybody loves everybody—and there is no possibility of a con game going on.

The Playbook says it is a place, according to Revelation 22:3–5 and Revelation 7:15–17, where there is:

1. Perfect Sinlessness
   "There shall be no more curse."
2. Perfect Government
   "The throne of God and the Lamb shall be in it."
3. Perfect Service
   "His servants shall serve Him."
4. Perfect Communion
   "They shall see His face."

5. Perfect Happiness
   "There shall be no night there."
6. Perfect Control
   "They shall reign forever and ever."
7. Perfect Closeness
   "They are before the throne of God."
8. Perfect Cooperation
   "And serve Him day and night."
9. Perfect Family-ness
   "He . . . shall dwell among them."
10. Perfect Satisfaction
    "They shall hunger no more, neither thirst."
11. Perfect Leadership
    "The Lamb . . . shall feed them and shall lead them."
12. Perfect Joy
    "God shall wipe away all tears from their eyes."

That is what the Playbook says about where Bill Betts went!
I am looking forward to being with him . . . where you don't
have to squirt passes out of a slick hand.

TWENTY-ONE

Mrs. Connell's Thera-pie

I am quite aware that I have been a dart pain in the glutei maximi of some very qualified, well-washed, overly insured Republican Bapti-Methodo-episcapo-funda-liberals, not to be confused with the Metho-Bap-terians.

When I was a boy, religion bothered me. In fact, it bothered everybody. There was a time, during my cynical period of adolescence (a condition which is required in the lives of all of us) when I wasn't able to abide the piety-possessed, and church-obsessed.

The Good Lord knows; they were hard to abide.

As my friend Tim Klussman said, "I grew up in a town that had only two churches. One of them thought nothing was a sin. The other thought everything was a sin. Unfortunately, I was a member of the church that thought everything was a sin."

I lived in a town like that and was a member of the "everything was . . ." church; and I lived in a state of constant dilemma because I dated a lovely girl who was a member of the "nothing was . . ." church. We each decided to witness to each other about why the other should join his/her congregation. We were highly effective in our witnessing because she joined my church, and I joined hers.

My reasoning for joining the other one was "To be a member of the church I am in is 'hell-now-heaven-later'. To be a member of her church was 'heaven-now-hell-later.' I figured out a plan: While I am young, I will be a member of the 'Heaven now' people; and when my glands die, I will join the 'Hell now' group." I suspect that this is the secret plan of many hot young bloods today.

There is nothing worse than the pycho-mishmash this philosophy engenders. To be constantly harassed by a church or a hot-collared, dyed-in-the-polyester pastor where you never can be good enough—or to be tut-tut-ed by a pipe-smoking, pink-faced, clucking liberal where the Dachau ovens are about the only thing God might wince at—is to be consigned to an anteroom to hell itself for the rest of your natural life.

These philosophies have provided a boom in the furniture business, because the sale of psychiatrist's couches has gone through the roof! It has made the victims of these excesses live in a "psychottage" (from which the psychiatrist collects rent) and these misanthropes rest in the shade of the old "psychia-tree," or walk down the oak-covered "psychopath."

Each of these ideas is obviously pathological.

Those who search the earth with a baseball bat for one small sin, so they can have the ecstasy of beating the bejabbers out of some poor frustrate, are deserving of nothing but aggressive opposition by the normal saints who walk the earth with joy written on their faces.

And, contrary to Hollywood's stereotypes, there are the love-joy-peace normal Christians who found happiness in the happy Christ, so clearly revealed in a normal study of the Jesus of the New Testament.

I believe, based on Asian humor, that there are at least a dozen laugh-lines in the Sermon on the Mount. If that scandalizes you, perhaps you are a member of the Quad-Sigs, "The Sacred Sorority for Snubbing Sinners."

The psychiatrists in those days were old women who just somehow knew that you needed someone to know, understand, and feel, so they would come over "because you looked like you needed a friend, Connie." Mother would cry and iron and iron and cry.

They would talk, and I would sit in a darkened corner of the room, and just listen, while Mrs. Connell, Mother's psychologist, patted her and they'd both cry, and mother would iron and cry and iron and cry. Then, suddenly, as if by signal, the session was over. Tears dried up immediately, and they would snap right out of it.

What pulled off this miracle healing from tears, problems, hurt, and hankering? It was time for Major Bowes, and the "Original Amateur Hour," the Eddie Cantor's Conoco Hour, the Fred Allen Show, and The Jack Benny Show.

Then they would turn off the radio, and Mrs. Connell would get up, saying, "Where did the time go?" Then, that sweet woman would do what I prayed to God she'd do. She would go out to her car, a Hudson, and take out a cake. I'll swear it was a foot thick. Banana cream pie cake.

It was then that I knew there was a God in heaven, the Holy Bible was true, and Jesus loved us all—through the tall, stately, lovely Mrs. Connell. Psychiatry, through banana cream therapie!

You talk about being seeker-sensitive. It was the Mrs. Connells of this world who brought people to Jesus.

I don't know how she lived without the feminist movement, and NOW. But somehow, she managed. If she could meet Mollie Yard or Gloria Steinhem, she'd bake them a cake and tell them that Jesus wants them to lighten up, sweeten up, and every time they feel like spouting off like Vesuvius, just stuff their face with Mrs. C's banana cake!

She knew what good Brother St. Francis meant when he said, "Preach the Gospel at all times. If necessary, use words." And we all will survive, if we will just get back to that reality of basic human honesty.

There was something about the Great Depression that cured us of interpreting life through our colored sociological glasses. We didn't need causes and banners and enemy lists or villianization of those who disagreed with us. We needed, quite simply, Western culture, rang eland honesty, and handshake contracts.

TWENTY-TWO

How to Have a Two-Armadillo-Jump Day

What is a friend? One who is interesting, entertaining, dependable, safe, encouraging, helpful, and warmth giving. I have many friends who meet nearly all of those qualifications—and a few who meet all of them.

Those are the people called "best friends." Doris and I classify Harold and Carolyn Kelham among the latter group. Harold is an affluent business executive. Carolyn is a stable, kind, motherly, but not-to-be-conned woman, who loves scuba diving and world traveling.

I am a storyteller. Storytellers seem to cluster; and Harold and I cluster good, as they say out on the Western range. One of my favorite Harold Kelham stories relates to his efforts to find a nice, quiet place for respite from the clutter and bang of life.

He bought a ranch at Leakey, Texas. It was the C B X O Ranch (the Clutter-and-Bang-Exxed-Out-Ranch). That wasn't the name of it. I just named it that to indicate its purpose.

Harold enjoyed sitting in the shade of his sumptuous ranch house—at first. After a few days, the joy of the experience sort of wore off. "I was looking for a place of peace and quiet," he said, "but I didn't know how peaceful and quiet and maddening just sitting there could become."

It became like the Buddhist nirvana, just doing nothing and being nothing for hours on end. Harold would walk around the house for entertainment, or just sit in a chair and watch the banana pudding turn black. Or he would sit outside in the shade and watch the grass grow, giving a name to each blade.

Harold related to me that his only diversion was watching armadillos wobble around him. On an average day, one armadillo would roll up to him, not having any idea that he was anything alive, since armadillos are nearly blind.

Harold said that, when the armadillo would get up close to him, he would jump up and yell, waving his arms violently. The armadillo can jump straight up, about two feet off the ground, when frightened like that. This was Harold's only diversion—watching the banana pudding turn black and scaring the bejabbers out of an armadillo.

Harold, a master storyteller, paused for the chuckled response. It wasn't a belly shaker. Just a chuckled response.

After a few seconds, Harold related that a really big day on the ranch was a two-armadillo-jump-day.

I lived in the clutter and bang of America for more than fifty years, swimming in the sea of sensates, gasping for breath, with people dying, divorcing, deceiving, and delusioning all around me. Then, I slowed down a bit, took up teaching at Southwestern Baptist Theological Seminary and Palm Beach Atlantic College, and preaching here and there.

It was a slowing down of the clutter and bang, to a faint whisper, just an occasional clank, ping, bump . . . and a joyous, uproarious two-armadillo-jump day. I really looked forward, with senile alacrity, to the special interruptions of those 2AJD's.

There just isn't anything like growing a little older, with baldness, bridgework, bifocals, bulges, bone aches, and bunions.

Did you ever notice how *little* older people can talk about? Usually, it is an organ recital: "My stomach . . . my liver . . . my bowels, etc."

I have learned something about the difference between complaining old people, and the really joyous ones. The really happy ones love to have, and tell about, their two-armadillo-jump days.

As I look back on my life, I don't understand why absolutely everybody doesn't go into the ministry. I mean really involved, fighting-the-devil-in-modern-Babylon ministry! There is no life with more involvement: One day, you are on the bomb squad, defusing a blockbuster situation. The next day, you are tearful as you have to tell a mother that her son has been killed in a wreck. Another day, you share the quiet gentleness of a beautiful Christ-honoring wedding. One 2AJD after another!

Jesus' life was a swirl of jumping armadillos. They crawled up on all sides of Jesus, and His words and actions sent every one of them two feet off the ground! See them jump!

Raising Jairus's daughter . . . and Lazarus . . . healing ten lepers at one time . . . changing water into wine . . . walking on water . . . preaching the Sermon on the Mount—and getting into holy hot water because of it . . . confronting the Pharisees . . . facing the soldiers' spears in the Garden of Gethsemene . . . feeling the *hack! hack! hack!* of the hammers, as nails were driven into His hands and feet . . . radiating the resurrection in the faces of those wide-eyed believers . . . ascending into heaven . . . and sending the Holy Spirit to shake up the whole world . . . then bridling up the White Horse for that Big Ride back to earth!

Jumping armadillos! So many armadillos jumping that Mars can feel it! Jumping all over the earth, and shaking up the heavens as well!

TWENTY-THREE

Hitler, the Skinheads, and a Surprise Visitor

He was a smallish, frightened child. There was every reason for fear to be his companion by day, and terror his bedfellow by night.

It was his father. The boy was given a whipping, sometimes a serious beating, every day. The sound of his father coming home caused the child to run to the back of the house; but the father knew all of his hiding places. The towering man demanded total respect and total obedience. The father insisted that the lad salute every time the father entered the room.

The mother was a good woman, but she was equally frozen at the sight and sound of her husband's imposing presence.

At the table in the evening, he would pontificate as the meal grew cold. His subjects consisted of injustices at the office, the sneaking, conniving people who ran the various businesses on the street, the ancient past glory of his country ruined by the present government. He ranted, fumed, raved, roared, screamed, pounded on the table, giving object lessons to the boy of what he should become, and how he should act when he became a man.

Every rant drove the boy more deeply within himself. Every scream played concerts on his nerves and grooved deeply into his brain. The pounding increased his fears, and decreased his self-image and self-belief. The boy's name was Adolf Hitler.

The child, Adolf, took all of his insecurities, doubts, fears, and anger, and bundled them together in a hard knot of gall and bitterness. This ball of gall was lodged in his psyche, emitting resentment and hate throughout his personality all the way from the time he was thirteen until the bunker.

Robert Browning was right—"The child *is* the father of the man." The child, Adolf, took all of his father's insecurities, doubts, and fears—and the demanding, screaming dictator was born.

We are not reincarnated, but there are many births *inside* our lives. That hard knot was born and lived inside young Adolf. The world suffered deeply because a neurotic child was not helped. Wouldn't it have been a wonderful thing if a church nursery worker, or a dear teacher, could have had an opportunity to reach him? What if his mother had gone to a ladies Bible class, which led her to Christ and guided her through the trials of young motherhood?

If someone had shown a way of healing to young Hitler, six million Jews and millions of Christians would not have died, and millions of Russians, Poles, British, French, and

Americans would be alive and walking free. Such is the importance of guiding one little life aright.

Apparently, Hitler had leadership ability, an almost satanic civility and charm that beguiled the very bright German people.

What if his father had found a Promise Keepers' meeting, or a brotherhood of Christian men to lead him? The entire world would have been different. A trillion dollars of this world's goods would have been saved. American manufacturing plants would have been built, paving the way for still further industrial development. Science would have funded projects for peaceful, healing pursuits, instead of destruction of life and property.

Now, consider deeply the next sentence.

Adolf Hitler, with his dynamism, was the same as the apostle Paul, without the Damascus Road conversion experience. Paul was a murderer, a bigot, seething and yeasting religious prejudice, walking about seeking every Stephen he could find, to have their bloody clothes laid at his misdirected feet.

"And the witnesses laid down their clothes at the feet of a young man named Saul [Paul]" (Acts 7:58 NKJV).

This Saul was a potential Hitler, a potential Karl Marx.

". . . On that day a great persecution broke out against the church at Jerusalem, and all except the apostles were scattered throughout Judea and Samaria" (Acts 8:1 NIV).

When Jesus was arrested in the Garden of Gethsemane, the disciples fled into the night; but the post-resurrection apostles lost the ability to run away, because they knew the rest of the story!

"He [Saul] laid waste to the church continually with cruelty and violence; and, entering house after house, he dragged out men and women and committed them to prison" (Acts 8:3, Amplified).

The lessons are clear. The worst person, without Christ, will become more intensely evil, if unchecked. There are laws of physics at work here. "Anything that moves causes friction."

"Any moving object, unchecked, will move in that direction forever."

"The longer an object moves, if there is a force pulling it, the more the momentum of the object."

Hitler was a moving object. The Christian churches were formal, ritualistic, unrealistic, lost in theological niceties, bathed in a culture that would not change, and without the courage to stand against Hitler.

Today, this is the greatest stumbling block in sharing our faith with the Jewish people. The Jewish people continually ask the question, "Where were the Christians when the ovens were blazing?" Recently, I was asked to speak at a Jewish temple in Encino that had been terribly defaced by Nazi-like skinheads, who painted swastikas beside their menorah.

I was overwhelmed that the temple members had told their rabbi that they would trust Loyd John Ogilvie and Jess Moody, two protestant ministers, to interpret the situation to them. When I arrived at the temple that evening, I was amazed at the love the packed congregation showed me. There was something else that stunned me even more. Standing around the room were the most intimidating small army of tattooed, black-leather-clad, muscled, bearded motorcycle gang members. The very sight of them sent a little fear clutch to my throat. My heart skipped several beats.

Who were they? What did they want? Why were they there? I asked the rabbi seated next to me what was happening.

"They are a gang of ex-Hell's Angels who have formed a Christian group. They are here to show their support."

I looked back at them. That army of bombastic giants had served notice that, whereas they once dealt misery to everyone who stood for good; they now have transferred their intimidation against the bigots of the world.

They later told me that they have the message out on the streets: "Skinheads, you don't have to face one little rabbi, whose temple you once defaced as night cowards. You now have to answer to us! Our motorcycles will ride in the night—so if we find you, we might have to ask our Lord for forgiveness for what we might do to you, before we lead you to Christ!"

Converted bigotry! Converted muscles! Converted tattoos! Angels from heaven instead of hell.

In a real way, we all should be heaven's angels. Should we not?

TWENTY-FOUR

Saint George of the Bells

It started—at the beginning—as an idea. Then the idea grew legs and began to crawl all over me until something was done about it.

God doesn't jump on me and suddenly whomp up a revelation. He sneaks in on the wings of a faint whisper. Then it grows louder, then louder. Until finally, I think I'm sitting inside a Salvation Army drum on State Street in Chicago on a Saturday night.

The only way I can stifle the blasting beat is to do what the Master Drummer demands. Well, the message of the drums was to start a little church up on Singer Island. Singer was alive with dead people. No church in an area always results in a dead-dog town.

I started by asking the government for *permission* to start a church in the area. I was told a flat *no*. (I could get off my subject and write ten volumes on city governments and how I consider them the worst forms of vermin on earth. But that is for another day and another book.)

As I felt the humiliation of the dressing down of their rejection, it could have killed the whole idea. The voice settled it for me when I was mulling the city vermin's un-American and unconstitutional no. "Do you work for them or for me?" the voice said.

So, I rented the large meeting room of the Sheraton Hotel on the beach. A man offered to help me make it happen. His name was George Schulmerich.

George was the CEO and owner of the Schulmerich Bell Company. They manufactured the beautiful carrilon bells that rang in church towers all over the world, as well as the lovely handbells used in churches everywhere.

"I'll help you, and I'll tell you why," he growled.

(That is what he did when he talked; he *growled* with a deep resonant growl.) "Not that I am a Christian—because I'm not. I just don't like to see !!XO**()?0! city governments run over people. Those little no good **!!()?!!XX0! using government to try to deny freedom of religion. My God—man, it is BOSTON TEA PARTY TIME!"

He shivered my timbers every time I talked with him. Actually, he used some of the same words I used in the pulpit. George just *arranged* them differently. I couldn't stomach his vocabulary, but I loved his spunk.

Others soon gathered around the idea of a new church on Singer: Zell Davis, a great lawyer, whose beautiful wife was a master pianist, stepped in to help.

Bob Winters, a kind, gentle—opposite of George—retired exec, was of immeasurable help. Bob was the only one who shared the same denominational ties as I. He was a trained, loving Baptist Christian.

George Schulmerich was Simon Peter: strong, boisterous, colorful of speech, a kicking donkey in a crystal glass shop.

Zell Davis was James, the apostle, practical to the core, winsome, a consensus-finder and smoother-over type person. We needed him with George in the room.

Bob Winters was John the apostle, a quiet, faithful, I'm-right-here-at-your-side guy.

There were others, who sort of came out of their condo cocoons on the ocean to help us build the little church on Singer Island.

We named it the Chapel in the Sun Church of West Palm Beach. So, the beginning of the little chapel was a second-mile love effort. I have discovered that God blessed the second mile much more than the first. It was a stretch to put up with this miniature polyglot society of speckled birds.

"What am I going to do with this bunch to make them into a cohesive fellowship?" Then I asked the question that was really haunting me. "Lord, what am I going to do with George?"

The Lord answered, helpfully, "Do the best you can."

"Thanks for Your invaluable help, Lord."

I took the tack Jesus took. He had a bunch of poor ragamuffins to work with, and He molded the twelve into an elite loving unit. But my group weren't ragamuffins with no self-image and no money. My group had money and iron egos.

They weren't ragamuffins. They were furamuffins. They didn't walk from place to place. They Jaguared. I Forded.

We started with more than a hundred people. I was elated. The little chapel was born. We set up a constitution and some bylaws. I can never forget the beginning of our first meeting to set up the constitution. We sat down at the long executive table; all of us feeling good about our beginning. I asked Zell to chair our first meeting. Zell, to whom I shall ever be grateful for his help and friendship, began the meeting with a few words of encouragement to several people for their help in starting the Chapel in the Sun.

Then Zell made a fatal mistake. He dropped the cookie jar right there. "We have been blessed so very richly, and I know we want to thank the Lord for his rich blessing upon all of us. With our hearts so filled with joy, let us all bow our heads, and examine our hearts. Brother Schulmerich, will you lead us in a little prayer of thanksgiving for making this all happen."

That's when he dropped the cookie jar. George sat bolt upright. "I don't pray any *!XoXX! prayers. Call on someone else!"

This wasn't quite like the tippie-toe-and-talk-nice deacons meeting we usually held at old First Baptist. Zell didn't bat an eye. He was a lawyer who had sat through scores of alligator meetings. He specialized in fur flying.

"Thanks, George, for your input. Brother Winters, would you lead us?"

Bob led us in a sweet-Jesus-thank-you-for-every-blessing prayer.

What most of these folks wanted was a church, the services of which contained several features. Mostly, they wanted a nice New England-type service with a Calvin-robed minister preaching the living Christ, a positive effervescing sermon, about twenty minutes in length. But the chief requirement was a well-timed benediction, honed and chiseled to perfection. The "Amen" had to be sounded not a second later than thirty minutes before tee off time at the country club.

It is the same situation as today in a Dallas church. I hear of pastors who are fired in the Dallas-Fort Worth area. Many excuses are given: "incompatibility," "philosophical differences," and a score of other substitute excuses. The real reason for pastoral firings there is that they break "The Rule" three times.

The Law of Medes and Baptists in the Metroplex (Dallas/Fort Worth area) is that the benediction must be pronounced at least one hour before the Cowboys' kickoff time. The Cowboy code is that if a pastor violates the code one time, he receives a severe public reprimand. If he violates it two times, his salary is cut by twenty percent, and access to getting Cowboy tickets is cut off entirely. This usually solves the problem for most pastors.

In the unbelievable event that it happens *three* times, he is summarily terminated, the fact is printed in *The Baptist Standard,* and usually the pastor is never heard of again. To lose one's church is bad enough; but denial of both actual attendance at the games, and being forbidden to watch it on television, has sent many pastors to mental institutions and a few even to suicide, called in Texas "Cowboyicide."

But back to George Schulmerich.

George was a *postinvocationist* and a *prebenedictionist*. This tugs for interpretation. He enters the worship service after the opening prayer, and leaves before the closing prayer. He was a slow-entrance Christian and a quick-getaway Baptist. Many people asked, as they stood in the swirling dust of his exodus, "Who was that masked man?"

Church worship became an increasing irritant for George. His attendance became more and more infrequent. Finally, he ceased attending. His rationale was that while he liked everybody, there was no sense in having a huge yacht with a beckoning ocean, and not using them.

George was like my old friend, Jack Faircloth, who named his yacht *A Deal* so that his secretary could inform those seeking him, "Mr. Faircloth is not in. He is out on *A Deal!*"

I offered George my hand. He would slap it away verbally. "I don't need it." . . . "I don't want it." . . . "I am not interested." . . . "I don't believe in it."

Finally, his lovely wife, Alice, came to me to express her concern for George's soul. "I love him dearly; but when it comes to Christianity, George toughens up."

I was struck by the grim irony that George's company was the world's leading manufacturer of church bells, yet he would be so much an advocate of stonewalling against Christ.

Once, I sat alone with George and Alice and listened to his endless litany against Christianity. I interrupted his deep-throated pontificating and pressed him. "George, old friend, please hear me. With all the love of my heart I want to tell you something." I looked him squarely in the eye. "You will never be happy until you give your life to Christ."

George snarled. I pressed on. "Only then, can you hear the bells in your heart." No response.

Later, Alice and I met in my study. There we nailed down a solid joint covenant to believe and claim the vital, conscious conversion of George to Jesus. Alice told George of our pact.

"You tell that preacher for me that he can *!0XX!"

I made up my mind that only serious prayer could unlock the corroded, rusted, hard-bitten, long history of rejecting God's call. Just about that time, I was called as the pastor of the First Baptist Church of Van Nuys, California. George and Alice were now far away; but they were never really out of my mind. Van Nuys was an immensely taxing, complex, and strange experience. I was confronted with "Californianism," a synonym for "Corinthianism." For every problem I had in West Palm Beach, I had ten in Los Angeles. Nothing is uncluttered there. The cultural level was far beneath that of the Palm Beaches. "If it weren't for bowling, there would be no culture at all in L.A." When I said that to my congregation, they didn't protest; they actually applauded. Los Angeles is a massive graveyard for slain egos, low ethics, moral turpitude, under-the-table-ism, and intrigue. This is especially true of its government. The whole place reeks of compromise.

It is no accident that the moral quality of movies made *outside* of Los Angeles is light years above that of those made inside of L.A. I differ from most sociologists and even my own Christian brethren who say that Hollywood has corrupted the city. I believe the city has corrupted Hollywood. That was the environment in which I was laboring—a far cry from West Palm Beach's quiet beauty and gentle people.

Many times I thought of and prayed for George. He was a strange amalgam of wonderfully loving humanity and raw-red earthiness. I had memories of him that were now pleasant and then horrendous. You could have a pleasant meal with him until you touched the Christ hot button and the detonation would have all the fallout of a Mount Saint Helen's. The dust-ash clouds would go seventy-five thousand feet up and hover for days.

One day I was in the absolute panic of office activity in Van Nuys when my secretary, Margaret Delbo, said, "There is someone here to see you. His name is George. He has a voice like a thunderstorm."

"It's George Schulmerich!" I said.

I was so pleased that George and sweet Alice had come to see us. I ran out to greet him. "George! Alice!"

"Hello, you old *!XX0?!"

The entire office staff sat bolt upright in that orthodox fundamental church. George's style went over like a pregnant high jumper with them. He seemed to be aware that his whole demeanor utterly dominated the atmosphere—for good or ill.

We went into our study.

"Alice, be a riddance. I'm gonna talk with Reverend Jess."

We sat down.

"George, I'm so glad to see you. Doris and I want to take you to a little restaurant—"

"Cut the crap, Jess. I'm dying of cancer. I don't believe there is anything to this Jesus stuff. I'll give you ten thousand dollars right now to deny Him. If you'll take it, I'll never tell anybody, ever. Ten thousand dollars. I've got it right here in my pocket. It's yours . . . I . . ."

"You can take your ten thousand dollars, which I would love to have and need, and give it to the nearest drunk on the street. You have insulted me, George. I want that money so much, it hurts; but I gave my life to the ministry because Babe, Gene, John Henry, David, Pryor, and John died in World War II. I can't take your money and I can't take your attitude. Now, George, you are my friend. Don't make me cram that money down your throat!"

George was livid.

"You !xx00?! I came all this distance to help you make it! I—"

"George, you have strained my resistance a hundred times before. I have been pressed by this church to the limit of my humanity. Now you show up with *this*. I can't take much more."

"Fifteen thousand dollars!"

He was taunting me.

"George, in the name of God, stop it!"

"Twenty thousand dollars!"

"You're a jerk. Stop!"

"OK, it's down to fifteen thousand dollars."

"Stop it!"

"Ten thousand dollars and last call."

"No."

"OK, let's go to that restaurant."

"George, you've offered money to me; now this is my offer to you—eternal life. You hear that? Eternal life? You are dying. I love you, you jerk! Eternal life! You'll never hear the bells—"

"Forget the meal. Alice and I are going back to Florida!"

He stormed out.

I followed him out to his car.

He and Alice got in the car, and started off in a cloud of dust.

"Eternal life, George!"

As the car drove off, George gave me the finger.

That was the last time I saw him.

A month later, I was at home having breakfast when the phone rang.

"Jess, this is Alice. George died last night. He told me just before he died to tell you something."

"What is it, Alice?"

"He said to tell you he could hear the bells."

TWENTY-FIVE

The Empty Room

It was Christmastime.

There were three children and Dad. Mother had died just two months before, of cancer. Dad had done everything he could to create the same sort of atmosphere that Mother was so good at: a toasty fire, Christmas ornaments put up just as she had done the year before. Her last picture at the center of the mantle. How were they to make it in such a difficult time?

Father had carefully worked out a plan, one that would challenge them. "We have an old room at the back of the house. I am giving each one of you a dollar. The one who can buy something that will fill the room will receive a special gift."

The oldest boy, Chris, bought a bale of hay. He threw the hay into the air, and it filled the room temporarily, but then it settled down.

"That's great, Chris," Dad said, "Now let's see what Sean can do!"

Sean, son number two, bought two old pillows. Eagerly, Sean ripped them open, and threw the feathers into the air, filling the room temporarily before they settled down.

The little daughter, Jessica, said, "Daddy, I may have done something wrong; but I gave a quarter to that old blind man, sitting on the street, playing Christmas carols on his harmonica. Then, I met two boys, whose clothes were tattered. They looked hungry, so I gave them each a quarter. Then, I took the last quarter and bought *this*."

She pulled out a small, red candle. One of the boys giggled. She lit it, and the whole room was full of light!

The father said, "Jessica wins. She filled the room with several things: light, love, hope, and wisdom."

Jesus came as the Candle of the Lord. He has filled the whole world with light, love, hope, and wisdom.

As the little group of four sat in front of the crackling, happy fireplace, Jessica knew *for sure, for certain*, that she could see Mother smiling through the entertaining, inviting fire. And Jessica started singing at the top of her voice:

Joy to the world, the Lord is come!
Let earth receive her King.
Let every heart prepare Him room;
And heaven and nature sing;
And heaven and nature sing . . .

Then, as with one voice, they all chimed in:
He rules the earth with truth and grace . . .
They all felt that Mother was right there with them, singing at the top of her voice!

TWENTY-SIX

Ron's Ghost

Freedom!

Men will die for it and lie for it. Men will sing of it and write of it. They will do everything for freedom—except define it. They love to wax eloquent concerning it, so long as the flowers of verbiage cover its ugliness and its difficulties.

Freedom!

How that word has been prostituted by those mesmerized by the wicked witch of Western theology galloping from the ivy jungle of New England and the three German brewmasters: Barth, Brunner, and Bultmann, whose concoctions were mostly foam.

The liberal advocates of vapor theology and sociology have made our schools into hoppers of illiteracy, our prisons into incubators of criminality, our judiciary system into grandmotherly mollycoddles, and our compassion into a rubberband morality that stretches all over the place.

This has resulted in a country as disorganized as choir practice in a mental institution. It makes as much sense as the Bee Gees singing *The Messiah.*

Freedom!

The average American knows nothing about freedom and responsibility, following the philosophy of *me-firstism,* an I-I relationship in which we love for our teachers and preachers to say that any *tiny* sacrifice is being too hard on ourselves; that's producing the human house carpeted with wall-to-wall marshmallows. This is the formaldehyde school of religion.

All right, America, isn't it about time that the Author of freedom be allowed a couple of lines in this modern Tower of Babel? Quiet on the set! Jesus speaks.

But there is one group that will not be silenced. It is the religious toward their own selves, who have all the answers and want no questions.

Jesus speaks up above this self-congratulatory group: "I am going away, and you will look for me, and you will die in your sin. Where I go, you cannot come. . . . if you do not believe that I am the one I claim to be, you will indeed die in your sins. . . . then you will know the truth and the truth will set you free" (John 8:21, 24, 32).

There is the root word to freedom—*free.* No freedom without free men. No man is free until he comes to the truth.

Then His voice rises higher as He shouts the verse that sets us free: "You will know the truth, and the truth will set you free" (John 8:32).

Pharisees can't understand this. Angry gossiping fundamentalists can't understand it. Hate merchants will not accept it.

Quilt spillers can't comprehend it. Only those who become little children can be open enough to hear the liberty bell ring in the soul. "Free indeed!"

When a Roman slave was freed there was a simple ritual. The slave stood between the master and a Roman citizen chosen to represent Roman freedom. All three stood before a magistrate.

The Roman citizen placed his hand upon the head of the slave and shouted, "This man is now free. I declare him to be free."

Then the slave spoke, "I wish to be free."

Then the master intoned, "This man now has no master!"

The magistrate then declared, "This man is free indeed."

And all around the room shouted, "Free indeed!"

Today a person—a slave to sin—stands before Jesus Christ. Jesus shouts when the sin slave repents: "This person is free indeed!"

Free indeed means free from past guilt, free from present domination, free from future punishment for sin, and free from the fear of death.

Secular people say they are not bound; therefore they do not need to be freed. They know they lie even as they speak because there is an impulse of truth from God's Word that connects directly to their inner bosoms, disturbing their rest, diverting their minds, and stealing their joys. The choice is yours: a slave in need or free indeed?

You are freed from some things and not freed from others. You are not free from the moral law. You are not under it as a covenant for justification, but you are under it as a rule of direction. You are not free from the temptations and assaults of Satan. You are free from his dominion, but you are not free from his molestation. He can't kill you, but he can afflict you. You are not freed from the motions of indwelling sin (Rom. 7:21–24). You are not free from sickness or the rods of affliction (Heb. 12:8). You are not freed from death's stroke, but you are free from the sting (Rom. 8:10).

Sin is un-freedom. Sin is un-life. Sin is un-joy. Sin is un-love. Sin becomes unbearable. Sin is uncouth.

The central lock in the chain of all slavery is sin. When it snaps shut tightly, only a key shaped like a cross can unlock it. The cross is the key to your freedom.

Recently I had dinner with Ron and Saundra Killough. I performed their wedding several years ago and we celebrated their anniversary together. Ron's is a terribly tragic but truly wonderful story. He is an inordinately handsome, quiet young man, who before he came to serve on staff with us in West Palm Beach, was the youth minister of the Woodlawn Baptist Church in Austin, Texas.

One Christmas, Ron was taking two busloads of young people to Glorieta, New Mexico, for a youth conference. You know how those bus trips are: singing, jabbering, counting off to make sure everybody was aboard, raucous laughter. The trip from Austin to Glorieta was long, and they were nearly there. Ron was in the front bus, feeling refreshed by the fact that they were only an hour or two away.

His reverie was broken by the cry of one of his young people, "The other bus didn't make it over the last bridge!" A large transport truck had collided head-on with the second bus!

Ron was the first on the scene. He saw the dead face of the music minister's wife, then her daughter, then the dying form of one of his teachers, and another, and another. More than twenty of them dead, everybody else injured, some very serious.

Ron worked for three hours trying to extricate bodies from the twisted wreckage, then spent several days comforting parents, preaching funerals, and counseling the remaining young people with their "whys." He ran just this side of total exhaustion. Later, the inner nightmare gnawed at his deeper life.

A few months after that experience Ron came on staff with us. We tried to help, but there is nothing quite so useless as proxy comfort. Ron's depression deepened. I prayed for Christ's specific help for him. Then I knew what I had to do. I called him into my study and said, "Ron, I want you to organize and lead our bus trip to Ridgecrest this July." The blood ran out of his handsome face.

"I'll try," he said softly.

That's all that was said. He organized the trip—actually overorganized it. That was the easy part. The hard part was that early Wednesday morning when the bus left. Ron stayed outside the bus until the last minute, organizing and labeling luggage, and talking with parents. He turned to me and said, "Pastor, do you want to lead them in prayer before we go?"

"Sure, Ron," I said.

At the end of the prayer, I stepped out of the bus and Ron stepped on board. It was probably the longest step he'd ever taken. As the bus drove away, I saw his face. It wasn't marked by terror, but it was the most grim countenance I had seen for a long time.

We prayed all week for Ron and the young people.

The next Friday, ten days later, the bus arrived back on the church parking lot. As the bus drove up, you should have seen guess-who smiling the broadest smile you ever saw.

Ron leaped off the bus, hugged and kissed his Saundra, hugged me, then went from person to person shaking hands like a politician the day before the election.

"I made it! I made it! Thank God Almighty! I made it!"

The Son had made him free. He can do the same for you. The chains don't have to bind you anymore. You can say, concerning whatever giant fear that grips you, "I made it! I made it! Thank God Almighty! I made it!"

TWENTY-SEVEN

Custerism

My domo prof at Southern Seminary and the University of Louisville, Dr. Wayne Oates, has the distinction of being the originator of a word that now appears in the dictionary. The word is *workaholic,* from Oates's book *The Workaholic.*

I want to try to coin a new word that describes an emotional and psychological condition, common to all mankind—at one time or another. The word is *Custerism.*

When the overwhelming flood of the sensate bombardment inundates the spirit and responsiveness drowns in the ocean of hopelessness . . . when the mind can't focus on any one object . . . when hope sinks to the bottom of the sea of despair . . . when life goes sour, and the bitter taste of it makes you want to call Dr. Kevorkian . . .

. . . you are suffering from *Custerism.*

Life thrives on hope, but you feel that the sense of the orphanage of the soul has taken up permanent residency in the chalet halfway up the mountain of glory. Hope is a sitting donkey, unwilling to be coaxed any further. Your thirst for meaning would give any possession to have but a half cup of hope to drink.

Hope sits in a faraway heaven, lost among the galaxies of infinite distance. To have hope is to have a clear eye that can see the glory of God, the mercy of Christ, the habitat of saints, and the angelic joys of paradise.

Faith is her attorney general. Prayer is her lawyer. Patience is her physician. Gratitude is her treasurer. Confidence is her vice admiral. The Word of God is her anchor. Peace is her companion. Eternal glory is her crown! When you are with her, Hope is the stars of Sisera, singing together.

The Grand Director, Christ, has all the instruments in life's orchestration in harmony and synch. And when you dance with hope, your feet are fleet, your soul sings to nature's unity, and the zing is zigzagging throughout the cathedral of the spirit. Man can live for a few seconds without air, a few days without water, a few weeks without food . . . but he can't live one flick of an eyelash without hope!

Now, let's move from the balcony of the poetic to the hot asphalt of the city streets. You know that life is a thousand Indians, and you are General George Custer when: *You have more war than you have troops.*

Hope has fled to the eastern hills when you are so far down that discouragement is a positive thought. Babies, bills, backaches, bulges, bifocals, bunions, and bridgework overwhelm you. The thought of prioritizing, the first law of order and decency, comes to mind; but it can't translate past your gasping, dying spirit.

You simply do not have the troops to fight that overwhelming battle. You plan to reorganize, but that requires order, and your life is disordered by unconfessed sin, unclaimed promises, and the unread Bible. You plan to calendarize, but the pages of time are burned out by the confusion of too many of the "Indians" breaking through too few of your defenses.

You know you are suffering from Custerism when: *It's too far from the battlefield to your supply lines.*

Financially, there is too much month at the end of the money. Legally, there is too much guilt without confession. Emotionally, there is no spiritual movement, because sorrow has paralyzed you. Visually, there is too much glare, and exposure has neutralized you. Intellectually, ignorance has limited your ability to cope. All this tragedy occurs because hope has fled to the eastern hills.

And all the while, Christ stands nearer than hands or feet—and you clasp His hand, or walk in step with Him.

You may have longed for the unrelatedness of Buddhism; or the absorption into nothingness of the Hindu nature, and the escape from this life to reincarnation. . . . But the hard reality of the God of the Ten Commandments beats you into "Just As I Am." And these other forms of escapism will not take you away from that Hound of heaven, Jesus, who doesn't *show* the way . . . but *is* the Way.

You find yourself ill-clad for what is taking place now. *You love your bright uniform in the parade—but not when the myriad eyes of the enemy are riveted upon you, and intent on your destruction.*

Your helmet has been pride; your breastplate, hatred. Your shield, excuses; your loins, lust. Your feet shod by the wrong cobbler, you've moved with swiftness to anger, to gossip, to sin. You must consult your battle manual, the Bible, and read Ephesians 6 for the proper battle attire.

Another harbinger of defeat: *The battle is too loud to hear the Captain's commands.*

Have you noticed how loud the battle of life has become? The din of sin roars in your ears, coupled with advertising's seductive siren song, then the sounds of the sensates, soaring above your ability to bear.

Joining these other problems is another. Will they never stop coming? I am encircled on every side. *My last option of escape has just been sealed off.*

The totally secular humanist book *No Exit!* by Albert Camus describes this form of *Custerism.* It gives no water to slack the thirst of the worst in humanity. Camus balanced a few intellectual probabilities, consulted only the rational powers of mankind, accepted no revelation from any God, anywhere, put his hand between himself and the sun, then denied the sun, looked outward only, denied the upward dimension . . . and came to the only conclusion such narrowness could reach: "There is no escape!"

He turned from Holy Writ, which clearly states, "There hath no temptation taken you but such as is common to man: but God is faithful, who will not suffer you to be tempted above that you are able; but will, with the temptation, also make a way to escape" (1 Cor. 10:13 KJV).

There are more Indians than I have bullets.

Carnal Christians can't compete when fighting the battle using carnal weapons. You simply do not have enough bullets in that carnal gun.

The Message paraphrases 1 Corinthians 3:1–4:

"But for right now, friends, I'm completely frustrated by your unspiritual dealings with each other and with God. You're acting like infants in relation to Christ, capable of nothing much more than nursing at the breast. Well, then, I'll nurse you since you don't seem capable of anything more. As long as you grab for what makes you feel good or makes you look important, are you really much different than a babe at the breast, content only when everything's going your way?"

You will be overwhelmed like a baby in a battlefield, like a squad against a division. You will be overcome on every side. Evil will swamp your defenses—because you insist on fighting in the field, without sword, breastplate, shield, or sandals.

The filling of God's Spirit gives you the advantage, but it requires full commitment on your part. The carnal Christian is a weaponless Christian, overwhelmed and swamped by the onrushing flood of secularism. The enemy outnumbers, outweighs, and outstrategizes you. You can't win, because carnality is sluggish, sottish, slippery, and sinful. It is too weighty for you to swim life's turbulent sea. You cannot make it unless you drop the carnality, embrace His forgiveness, and claim His filling! But it can be done by all and anyone—and that includes *you.*

These Indians won't reason with me.

The word *Indian* was Custer's well-earned problem. His troops had shot and knifed their children, wives, and old people. What the Indians did was totally understandable.

The forces of revisionism, secularism, and toleration of sin are totally unreasonable. There is only one answer for them—convert them to Christ, who will change them and give them ears to hear.

There is no reason to waste our time on the totally unreasonable persons. God give them eyes to see, and ears to hear!

My fears are overwhelming me!

You are crowded in on every side. Paul felt the smothering of that feeling. He was pressed on every side, but not discouraged. God had delivered him from all his fears. Courage was his constant companion.

"And when Silas and Timothy had come from Macedonia, Paul was compelled by the spirit, and testified to the Jews that Jesus is the Christ" (Acts 18:5, NKJV).

"For we would not, brethren, have you ignorant of our trouble which came to us in Asia, that we were pressed out of measure, above strength, insomuch that we despaired even of life" (2 Cor. 1:8, KJV).

Paul felt surrounded, hounded, and grounded—but his spirit abounded!

Our nation is far gone right now. We must learn that our strength is not in our armies, navies, or marines. Our strength is not in our oil fields, our far-reaching Internet, our great highway systems, banks, agriculture, mines, lakes, or educational institutions. The Bible is our greatest national asset!

It is supernatural in origin, divine in authorship, infallible in its authority, inexhaustible in adequacy, a miracle Book of diversity in unity.

The Bible . . . infinite in scope, universal in interest, eternal in duration, personal in application.

The Bible . . . inspired in its totality, regenerative in power, inestimable in value.

The Bible . . . unsurpassed in literary beauty, unequaled in simplicity of expression, immortal in its hopes, the masterpiece of God.

The Bible!

What they taught me at West Point doesn't work here in the white-hot heat of battle.

I was flying with some friends when our nose wheel went out. The landing would prove to be quite unpredictable. We called the manufacturer on the patched-in phone on the plane. After a lengthy discussion, the manufacturer's representative gave us these discouraging words, "I have nothing to suggest. Good luck!"

There is no hole to hide in, and no soul to confide in. Just pure trust in the sovereignty of a loving, caring Christ. He saw Peter through his crisis in the storm. He'll see you through all doubt and harm!

I wish I were an Indian named Small Snail.

It is better to be a small Indian alive than a great general dead!

That thought must have crowded Custer's mind; but it must not live in the Christian's heart. Compromise only prolongs the agony, and the latter state is more deadly than the first.

It is too late to use positive thinking.

Though thinking positively has its place, it is not an option when there seems no way out. Positive thinking will help one think through a dilemma, but this takes time—and when you are in a "Custer situation," there is no time.

The problem arises when there is no time to think through, wade through, triumph through, or bluff through. Such positivism is extremely helpful when there is time. There are situations, however, when there is no time—there is no exit—but upward.

A beautiful thing in the Scriptures appears in the death of Stephen. All through the Word of God, when referring to Jesus' intercession, He is spoken of as seated at the right hand of God. . . . Seated. . . . But when His heroic deacon Stephen was being stoned, and very near death, Stephen looked up and saw Jesus standing up, honoring his faithfulness, and moving to receive him. Stephen, breathing his last breaths, shouted skyward: "Lord Jesus, receive my spirit!"

So, now, while you are not pressed in from every side, while the waters of doubt and fear are *not* assailing you . . . now is the time to give everything you are and have into the hands of the living Christ. He holds all your tomorrows, all the future *Custerizing* experiences, all the hemming in—all of it is in His capable hands. If God can make Adam out of dust, just think what He can make out of what is left of you!

There are more things to deal with than there are brain cells to cope to do it.

The "Indians" encircling you are the sensate bombardments of this media sea engulfing us. Marshall McLuhan, the great father of interpreting modern media, told me that a sensate was any stimulus to the mind and spirit that was *designed* by man and purposed to cause man to redirect his originally intended course.

McLuhan asked me the year of my father's twentieth year, my twentieth year, and my son's twentieth. I told him that the years were 1922, 1945, and 1964. He astounded me by citing the approximate amount of sensates that each of us has to face.

1922 = 800–1,000 spd (sensates per day)

1945 = 1,200–1,600 spd

1964 = 18,000–30,000 spd

Then, McLuhan added the astounding fact that the human organism cannot thrive, and perhaps even survive, above 12,000 spds! "Man is mushing along with a massive overload on his psyche," he said.

This predicts a rise in the necessity of quietism, meditation, and any activity, or inactivity, that cools the spirit. This explains the reaction to hell-fire, damnation preaching, which infers heat—when only McLuhan's "cool" will suffice. Unless Christianity can accommodate this, there may be a massive move toward the Asian religions.

Christianity has thousands of verses that cool the mind and spirit, but they are dormant unless emphasized. Right at this point there is a great opportunity for "cool evangelism." Since we are drowning in mind-clutter, Christ—as Savior—takes on new meaning.

The Bible takes on importance, if one realizes the truth: If the mind of God gave you the Bible, then when you read the Bible, you are reading the mind of God. It is the mind of God in print, therefore—when everything is a clutter—read the Bible. It will unclutter you, cool the jets of the sensates, and change you from a mental and emotional mess into a message.

I will start the rain dance, and they will think I have been converted to become one of them.

This never works.

From the days of Simon Peter, warming himself by the devil's fire, having his mind penetrated by the message of the rooster-prophet, compromise has never worked. The evolution is ever downward, like the second law of thermodynamics, it wears downward, downward, downward.

It was first, in the Scriptures, "For Demas is with me" (2 Cor. 4:14). Then, simply "Demas" (Philem. 24); then, pathetically, "Demas hath forsaken me, having loved this present world" (2 Tim. 4:10, KJV). Demas's rain dance was a hell dance—a firestorm!

There is no escape from Custer cluster by compromise.

I would trade all my medals for one more day of life.

Come, lay all your medals down at the feet of Jesus, take up your cross, and follow Him!

TWENTY-EIGHT

The Ritual

My father was not a Christian at that time; but I heard him say several times, "There's one Christian in this town that I know of—and it's Joe Grizzle. When he walks by, take off your hats boys, 'cause he's got the good Lord in him."

Grizzle came by Dad's cafe regularly to see if Dad was ready to repent and give up selling 3.2 beer.

"Horace, when are you going to repent, follow Christ, and give up 3.2?"

"Joe, I would join your church; but there are too many hypocrites down there."

"Aw, come on down, H. F., there's always room for one more! You can't take it with you; and—if you could—it would have to be fireproof!" They would laugh.

It was a pattern repeated many times, a pastor-sinner joke just between the two of them. Later, my Dad would sit alone at the end of the counter, with a deep, pensive look on his face. He didn't want to be bothered.

"Grizzle's words always puts him in those deep fits of thought," Mother would say.

The respect for ministers, women, and children ran deep in those days. The country won't survive unless we get it back. Sometimes, when I am not being eaten alive by big city-itis, I think about those days—when we all got in the car to go buy gum, or watch the speedometer turn to 30,000, or just bunch up for bunching up's sake.

I see my dear mother's sweet face, and my dad's eyes catching hers, and a love stream flowed between them. And I know that even if the stars fell, or Oklahoma was hairlipped, and Arkansas mildewed, that my daddy loved my mother . . . and they both loved me.

That's a better child therapy than Freud, I'll tell you. The encompassing love I felt surrounding me carried me through some unbelievably tough times in later years.

Home was spelled w-a-r-m; family was spelled h-o-p-e; we didn't have two dimes to rub together, but *we* could rub together, and hug, and just be. It's that *just being* that people don't have much of these days.

There was no TV, the movies were clean and cost fifteen cents. I got in free, because Mother played for the silent movies for a dollar a night. When talkies came in, it put a real crimp in our economy, I can tell you.

TWENTY-NINE

The Man Who Changed the World

The historians missed it. The encyclopedias have it down wrongly. A Russian inventor, Vladimir Zworykin, is officially given the credit. Yet the scientific community is beginning to awaken to a fact that might revise their evaluation of it.

What is *it?*

Television.

Zworykin gets the credit for inventing it.

Philo P. Farnsworth did it; but he may never receive that designation because he had a problem that caused him never to receive the plaudits for his astonishing accomplishment.

The apostle Paul said something about it. Prejudice may have stood in the way—because of Farnsworth's "problem."

Farnsworth worked on a farm, plowing a straight line on a potato farm; yet his mind was far away, thinking through the electronic puzzle as to how to transmit moving pictures through the air. Here he was, a person with no electronic training and no engineering background. Also, he was completely out of step with the entire scientific world as to how to go about seeking a solution to the large enigma.

Coupled with his problem, no one was giving him even a moment's notice to be seriously considered as a contender in this frenetic chase to find the answer to photographic transmission without the aid of wires to interconnect between sending and receiving the visual transmission.

The scientists in London, Moscow, and New York had been struggling to find the solution to this dilemma, and they were aided by large grants that enabled them to pursue every avenue of research to solve it. So, what chance did this Farnsworth have, a potato farmer with no education in the sciences, and with his problem plaguing his every step?

While plowing, he imagined a different approach. He imagined dividing a screen into long rows. Just like the field he was plowing, using electricity to create areas of light and darkness at each point along the row. Then stacking the rows on top of each other, he imagined that they could bring to focus a picture.

Bingo! The results were better than anything the world of science had ever conceived. It is the very system used today.

Farnsworth struggled all his life to receive credit for his marvelous invention—but he never received historical credit, mainly because of his problem. What makes this story even more incredible is that Farnsworth was born in a log cabin. One can see the makings of a whole chapter in the future history books, but Farnsworth's problem denied him his limelight.

He had a propensity toward science, a completely logical left brain, a vivid imagination from his right brain, coupled with a photographic memory. His mind could analyze automobile malfunctions, electric battery chargers, and just about any mechanical concept imaginable. Yet, he would only now be recognized, because people have come to see that his problem was not a hindrance. The problem lay in the prejudice of others regarding his problem, not in the problem itself.

When he was eleven years old, the Farnsworth family moved to Idaho's Snake River. This delighted him because there they had electricity, which was the main seed fertilizing his mind to seek "wonder after wonder and every wonder true," as Saint Brude said.

In the attic of the old house, he discovered reams of old scientific magazines and journals. He spent endless hours devouring those publications, feeding his "dream machine."

The years came and went, and young Farnsworth tinkered with ideas that made his peers think of him as somehow "wacky on science," the oddball in his society.

As he read of the scientific search concerning sending moving pictures through the air, instinctively, he knew they were on the wrong track. He became enthralled with his study of the electron. Science was seeking some moving parts as a key to picture transmission. Philo Farnsworth knew better—but no one would listen, mainly because of his problem.

The girl who later became his wife, hesitated to marry him, because he would become ecstatic talking about moving pictures flying through the air, space travel, and assorted electronic wonders.

An inspiring teacher, Justin Tolman, patiently listened as the boy wrote his theories of light-picture movement through the air. He almost covered the chalkboard with his theories. Later, after the discovery, Farnsworth reminisced that it was Tolman's encouragement that fired up his determination to continue, in spite of his interfering problem.

Two businessmen, George Everson and Les Gorrell, took special interest in Farnsworth's ideas. They each invested their entire life savings in Philo's research. They overlooked his problem, showed faith in him, putting a total of twelve thousand dollars into his inventive genius, a lot of money in those days.

Farnsworth moved to Los Angeles and feverishly worked day and night, quickly using up the investors' money; but they never lost faith in him, and borrowed twenty-five thousand dollars to control the feverish race against the other inventors of the world.

He perfected the instrument, filed for a patent, which was refused until they could prove that it worked. So, on September 7, 1927, Farnsworth transmitted history's first electronic television picture, by sending the picture of a glass slide with a straight line in it from one room to another. Farnsworth had done it!

David Sarnoff, then president of Radio Corporation of America, sent the Russian scientist Vladimir Szworikin to visit Farnsworth, who naively told him everything about the invention. Sarnoff took the invention, heralded the Russian as the inventor, and spent huge sums of money announcing it to the world.

Farnsworth never received credit for his invention until many years later, 1957, on the game show *I've Got a Secret*. He was paid eighty dollars for appearing.

It was there that Philo Farnsworth revealed to an audience of forty million people not only his invention, but also his problem. He summed it all up in one sentence. "I invented electronic television when I was fourteen years old." His problem was his extreme youth.

The apostle Paul recognized the same problem when he said, "Let no man despise thy youth" (1 Tim. 4:12, KJV).

Later, as an old man, Philo sat with his wife, Pam, and watched as man made "one small step for man; one giant leap for mankind." Man had set foot on the moon, just as Philo, a bright boy, had told her when he was courting her. And it was on worldwide television.

"You know, Pam," he said, "it makes it almost worthwhile."

THIRTY

On Being Down
to Your Last Blanket

When I was a child, I had a "thou place." Especially on chilly mornings, and very especially on chilly, rainy mornings, I loved to sit in the bay window of the living room of our little home out at the edge of Littlefield, Texas.

It was particularly delicious to my ten-year-old mind to press my face against the glass and let the raindrops course down the other side of the glass and pretend it was pouring into my eyes, mouth, ears, and drooling all down my body. The enjoyment of the reality without the price of being soaked was, as I said, quite delicious. I loved to feel the chill and the image of wetness on one side and the friendly warmth of the fireplace on the other.

This is something modern science hasn't discovered, even now—half a century later: the formula for the magic of the mind. Technically, it reads C+BW+CRD=DM (child+bay window+cold rainy day=dream machine).

In the context of that wondrous glow, books took on a special meaning. I read *Big-Little* books (anybody remember them?), *G-8 and His Battle Aces, Zane Grey*, and scores of other wonder stabbers of boys' mental images.

There are two books, lost in some ancient attic or burned by some heartless, brainless, insensitive idiot—or some kind of old man who decided one day to clear out the clutter—I would pay dearly to have at my side again. The bay window has moved from the house to my tummy, but the books would be just as yummy if they were here with me now: *Italian Children's Stories* and *History from the Indian Viewpoint.*

Reading the Italian book made we want to be Italian, a boy living in Naples, or out in the mountains overlooking the blue Mediterranean. The Indian book made me keenly conscious of injustice and caused me to hate bureaucratic, legalized thievery done by politicians—well educated and crafty—overwhelming the uneducated Indian who had owned the land for centuries.

I remember the sense of hurt and moral outrage as I sat beside the chilly glass window and read a speech by an Indian chief, delivered before Congress in the late 1800s.

I wish I could find it, hold it, reread it, and preach it on national television today. That boyhood wonder book would shake us up, I'll tell you! The chief spoke quietly and with dignified eloquence before a hushed audience about the vast land holdings his people once held, before the days of reservations, which he called a sop to the conscience of the white man. He spoke of roaming free for days and still having days of land ahead of him.

Then, the white man began reducing their holdings—first a piece here, then many acres there, and miles and miles of beautiful land, until he said, "All I have left is my sleeping blanket. Here, white man, please take this and you will have it all."

He dropped the blanket and slowly shuffled his sandaled feet across the congressional floor. It was said that the sound of his walking was the only sound in the room—but it was a roar in the ears of their consciences.

That story struck in my mind—and lives in my heart today.

The years have come and gone since those happy days of swinging for hours in memory's hammock, but I still remember the euphorian fog that clouded out all the world's cares and thoughts of school, lessons, thinking about sitting up straight, kissing old aunts I didn't remember ever seeing before, and making sure my shirttail was tucked in.

It was the essence of the good life to have a bay window all your own that not even President Franklin Delano Roosevelt had curled up in, or Bing Crosby or Buck Jones, or Guy Lombardo, or even distant famous cousin Will Rogers.

I had my own special resting place, and nothing felt so grand, so luxuriant. It was better than a hot summer day and three Eskimo Pies all to myself with no relatives, friends, or neighbors with whom, in the name of Christian charity, to be required to share them. A unique resting place . . . all mine . . . all that summer day long.

When you have your own place, your very own, there is no sense of exile, of loneliness, of orphanage. You are home.

Jeremiah knew what it was to lose that. He wept the tears of long separation: "My people hath been lost sheep: their shepherds have caused them to go astray, they have turned them away on the mountains: they have gone from mountain to hill, they have forgotten their resting place" (50:6, KJV).

Mike Douglas asked me a question on his show one time: "What is the predicament of modern man, as you see it?"

I don't know why I answered as I did. It sort of came out, as spontaneously as a hiccup: "Man is running out of resting places." He is. He is crowding out the golden from the landscape of the soul. The lake of his spirit is no longer reflecting the mountain peaks of his idealism, and there are no greening woods of spiritual growth, pointing long sequoia fingers to the glorious Creator. So, he is losing cope power.

This morning I had breakfast with a world-famous human being. He is so wealthy he could write a check and the bank would bounce, but—somehow—the choir has stopped singing in the cathedral of his spirit. Money has ceased to enamor; fame has lost its kick. There is a dark brown taste in the roof of his psyche. He is heaven starved and can't feel the throb of thrill upon hearing words like *home* and *love*.

His spiritual telescope is out of focus because he is numbered, faceless, and lives in penthouse 2-B, Secular City, USA, on the late, great, planet earth.

I remember another bay-window book I loved to read. It was the poems of Robert Service. No decent self-respecting boy of ten would have dared be without his Robert Service poems. They were rich with identification and longing for the surging of your own red blood.

> I'm scared of it all; O, afar I can hear
> The voice of my solitude's call!
> We're nothing but brute with a little veneer,
> And nature is best after all.
> There's tumult and terror abroad in the street,
> There's menace and doom in the air.
> I've got to get back to my thousand mile beat;
> The trail where the cougar and silver tip meet,
> The snows and the campfire,
> With wolves at my feet;
> Good-by! For it's safer up there.
> To be forming good habits up there;
> To be starving on rabbits up there;
> In your hunger and woe;
> Though it's sixty below,
> Oh, I know it is safer up there!

But we know that a seething, restless soul cannot find peace in the street or some long-forgotten valley behind some undiscovered hill, a thousand miles off any man's map. The soul that is restless will be restless no matter where it is.

Then how can I bear the test and find the needed rest which cries in my troubled breast? It is really tough to keep on walking when we don't understand. When man and God both say no, how do we find the go to go and go and go? I must find the secret principle of what tires the soul. I must avoid the things that clip the wings of the inner eagle spirit. The body becomes weary from overuse; the soul becomes weary from underuse.

Ignore the soul and it will moan and cry and be a weariness to the flesh, even unto death. Nothing can make you happy when your soul is unhappy and undernourished because of the famine for the Word of God.

Now that I am a man-child and have no bay window into which to snuggle, I can seek my last blanket by looking back at some of the soul quotes that God gave me while living in the wonder of this past year. These are some thoughts God gave me that I have found to be true in the years of ministry. They are distillations from the crucibles of experience and pain. I give God full credit for them, because they usually came to me when I was too tired to think!

"A God, who can break the very measuring of time by the birth of one small baby in a lesser town like Bethlehem, can meet my needs."

"The greatest teacher is quiet listening."

"In the garden of God, difficulties and delays are the atmosphere in which He grows His miracles."

"God has a reason, based on His better sense, for every NO."

"Nations have cracked at the spine, in one day, when God's fulfillment time comes."

"When you don't know what to do, ask two questions: What is moral? and What would mother have me do?"

"I may have been born French, English, and Cherokee; but I have been reborn brother-of-all."

"The key to life is the joy of the travel, not the relaxation of arrival."

"If there is no challenge and purpose in heaven, I have no yearning for it."

"As I contemplate heaven, I assume that everything I have learned here is relevant there."

"While on earth, we cannot see Jesus for the storm; while in heaven, we cannot see the storm for Jesus."

"In the last two thousand years, what scientific fact has been dug up to prove Christ untrue?"

"The sixties shattered our rose-colored glasses; the seventies put in the prescription lenses; and just when everything seemed ready, the eighties went blind."

"It is almost impossible not to believe in a loving God who is like Jesus Christ. The atheists had to distort that image so they could deny Him. This is proof of their intellectual dishonesty and their predisposition to doubt."

"Some people have such terrible tempers, they could start a fight in an empty room."

"A man alone is a flickering match. A Spirit-filled group is a bonfire."

"Great congregations have grown beyond tribal worship. There is difference between a praising worship of a godly throng and an army of Pavlov's dogs, barking and echoing the Pastor's shibboleths."

"Doubt blocks the top of the well and announces that there is no water."

"Always be drawing larger maps."

"To have faith is to be in labor."

"Don't be so bitter that when you have a gall bladder attack, the doctor will rule that it acted in self-defense."

"A good doctor merely makes it possible for the sickness and the healing to get together."

"A physician who sees a correlation of body and spirit knows a shortcut to healing."

"What can't be, ain't; but that doesn't mean what ain't can't be."

"Always be looking for the eternal fitness of things."

"Time always works on the side of the man of God."

Before we took the recess to ponder a few quotes, I was thinking of how people come down to their last blanket. They will roar out by faith or whimper out like a retreating, frightened puppy, backtracking in abject fear. And some come to the place of nihilistic apathy.

When I think of that, I am reminded of the actor, George Sanders. He was the urban sophisticate who swam in the warm bath of favorable publicity for thirty years; he was married to a psychic prop of a woman who was democratically lusted after by men in Europe and America. She dined and wined with leaders of a score of discipline; enjoyed Sanders's money and always had money to enjoy.

George Sanders died by his own hand. His bones bleach in the crypt; the mouth and eyes of the famous man are filled with dust. His terribly British accent will no longer echo in theaters and TV sets, except in the reruns. The eyebrows will arch no more in feigned disdain of the "little people" around him.

He summed it up in his suicide note: "I'm bored. I've lived long enough."

Back to the bay window, reading Robert Service:

> There's men that somehow grip your eyes
> And hold them hard like a spell.

George Sanders was one of those: actor, raconteur, dead man, and perhaps a soul in hell because of the hell in his soul.

The empty bottle beside the cold, famous corpse lay there at his fingers as a tiny prophet of the jading of the fading of the senses. One of those who couldn't make it and couldn't take it. Little empty pill bottle, what a message you preach to these victims of the sensate bombardment! These who die of cope fatigue, who lay down their last blanket.

THE SPELL OF THE YUKON

> There's gold, and it's haunting and haunting;
> It's luring me on as of old;
> Yet it isn't the gold that I'm wanting,
> So much as just finding the gold.
>   —*Robert Service*

JUST THINK!

> Just think! Some night the stars will gleam
> Upon a cold, grey stone,
> And trace a name with silver beam,
> And, lo! 'Twill be your own.
> The night is speeding on to greet

Your epitaphic rhyme.
Your life is just a little beat
Within the heart of time.
A little gain, a little pain,
A laugh, lest you may moan;
A little blame, a little fame,
A star gleam upon a stone.
                              —*Robert Service*

There are all sorts of deaths. I tell people contemplating divorce that there is but one cause of the death of a marriage—boredom! There is but one cause of housewife depression—boredom! There is one cause of executive fatigue—boredom!

When life becomes the yawn of a sinking sun instead of the dawn of a rising one, and little can calm and comfort the savage beast, boredom invades the crevices of the mind and rusts the hinges of the soul. When heartbeats seem heavy and even spacewalks seem like a fall stroll in a misty forest, life becomes so same, so same. . . . When your hankerer won't hanker and your wanter won't want, and your last merry-go-round ride ends up a thrilless exercise, and all of life tastes like the last sickening sweet bite of cotton candy, the temptation to run becomes oppressive . . . and a little Winnebago looks better than life's winepress.

When the hero in your soul has been slain by disillusionment and the Rubicon no longer beckons, or the test tube has lost its challenge, and your great novel is now not even a short story, then, you must find someone to whom to transfer blame . . . and if no spark comes from the dark and the bleak goes to black night, you need to hear anew:

"I am the Light of the world . . . I am the Light of this world's darkness . . . I am the Love of this world's hate. I am the Lord of this world's humanity . . . !"

Ah, little pill bottle, this frustrated, neurotic world must choose you . . . or the living, loving Christ!

Christ is my unboredom!

Suicide is the result of too many yawns, too many yeses, and too many strokes of sin's brush that paints the golden from your life's canvas and changes your brilliant sunset into a cold, rainy-day grey.

Every deed you do that is rebellious to Christ's cause is an investment in future boredom, in unliving. Then you are down to your last blanket. At that time in your life, only Christ can be your warmth.

THIRTY-ONE

Brother Joe F. Grizzle

God used images of the past for future reference—usually by putting a significant other in your life. God knew it would take a lot to get me into tow, so he put several of those "others" into my path.

The first big one, other than my folks, was Brother Grizzle, a man who truly felt that God almighty had held a conference in heaven and carefully planned his conception and birth so he could be the pastor of the First Baptist Church of Littlefield, Texas, in the 1930s.

I didn't think God even knew that there was a Littlefield, Texas; but Joe Grizzle knew for sure that God had planned it so that Moody's Cafe would be on the east side of the street, next to Sam Rumback's bakery.

This sort of thinking was needed in those days. Life was limited diminution. The only democracy we ever had was that everybody was equally broke. The best business in town was a used clothing store. We had no TV and few radios. The *Lamb*

County Leader, our newspaper, consisted of 4-H Club, Business and Professional Women's Club, and the Woodman of the World reports along with a few betrothees and funeral accounts. Nobody was ever quoted because nobody ever said anything. Life was symbolized more than verbalized.

But back to my significant other.

Joe Grizzle walked around town with that conservative look on his face, like somebody anticipating a firecracker about to go off. He knew that no one would appreciate grace if he didn't know what sin was. So he illustrated it on Sunday and incarnated it all week.

Few people could stare down my Dad. Grizzle would burst into Dad's cafe and say full voiced: "Get saved, Horace!"

Dad didn't duck, but you could tell he wanted to.

Grizzle would bore in, seeking gold. "Old man Carnahan ain't going to eat any more of your chili!"

"Why not?" Dad replied with concern. When you have precious few customers, you treasure every one of them.

"Cause he died this morning. So will you, one of these days."

"How old was he?" Dad questioned.

"Eighty-five."

"At eighty-five, you're s'posed to die. Come on in and eat his bowl—on the house."

That is as near to tithing as Dad ever got, until much later.

Grizzle's sermons had volume like a bagpipe in a phone booth. When he preached, it shook the chandeliers—of the Methodist church two blocks away. He was a soul rocker in the house of high holiness. He was, at once, in the moment, the movement and the mansions above, riding unshod and roughshod down the golden streets. If he didn't splatter mouth droolings fifteen rows back, the unction wasn't on him that day. There were no dull, droll, dozing of docile deacons in his domain.

His sermons were more exhilarating to his low-sensate world than "ER," "Chicago Hope," three soaps, and four game shows thrown in. You caught the spirit that was the equivalent of a Shell Oil explosion next door to Three Mile Island. He was one of those pyrotechnic preachers who sent the whole town to the bomb shelters. He preached as though I were Jewish and he was a terrorist bomber.

Joe Grizzle was God's man, truth on the move, who sent Satan scurrying from his scriptural sabotage. He never kept his convictions in a concoction of continual chloroform. He was the kind of pulpit Uzi who gave out perfect attendance pins, along with Purple Hearts. This pastor considered his whole day lost if he hadn't scandalized the bejabbers out of at least one eschonched saintly blissful Sabbath morn. His convictions were always ever near our central nervous systems. He could make a cadaver shudder.

Joe Grizzle was the exploding cigar in the face of condescending apathy and sin. Where sin abounded, Grizzle would bound around it until everybody was dying for a little grace. But Grizzle was good-hearted. Just when you thought there was no "therap" in this therapy, he would dispense grace, salvation, peace, and faith by the bushel barrel. If you weren't saved, you came to the place where you would kill for just a snort of it, to give you peace. Grizzle knew what he was doing and sincerely believed what he preached.

I remember when Grizzle got on the trail of Uncle Hardy. Hardy had the jake-leg and was easily treed. There was no way Uncle Hardy could get the fly-paper Bible-banger off his burdened back.

"That Grizzle is more cop than preacher," Hardy said. "He will bust you for breathing! Or for not grieving 'bout what was grieving him."

Grizzle could live quite close to one's nervous system; and there he would camp until you knew God was calling, and would keep on ringing until you answered the phone.

THIRTY-TWO

I Was the Miami Dolphins' Secret Weapon

For several years I served as a chaplain for the Miami Dolphins in the era of Larry Czonka, Jim Kiick, and Mercury Morris. I believe it was the greatest team of all time, coached by perhaps the greatest coach of the era, if not of all time, Don Shula. There was an almost perfect balance of bruising power, artful passing, quick opening tackles, and broken-field quickness. To my knowledge no team has ever gone undefeated in all history.

I am a minister. I deeply desire to be humble. But I must make an announcement. Czonka was sensational, perhaps the greatest power runner of all time. Tacklers bounced off him like billiard balls falling bewildered and broken at his feet.

The line, with great offensive effectiveness, and the likes of Norm Evans opening holes that a truck could drive through, then Czonka and Kiick picking the bones of the opponents bleached white.

Bob Griese, one of the master technicians of signal calling of all time, paved the way for victory after victory for the mighty Dolphins. Sports analysts have debated the reasons for the Dolphins' success. But, keen as they are, they have missed the *real* secret for their resounding victories. It is difficult for me to say it, but truth is truth—you can't change the truth, no matter how overlooked the real truth sometimes may be. I have a deep conflict in my soul telling this; but sooner or later some sports historian will discover it, so I am outing it, here and now: I was the real secret of the mighty Dolphins.

Don't laugh me to scorn. Hear me out. You, dear reader, are discovering the cloistered secret for the first time. I will now reveal it to those who are waiting with bated and unbated breath. Now do not misunderstand. The Dolphins were fantastic, fleet, and foreboding—but I *did* have a mighty and effective technique. There is a golden reason for the Dolphins' literally trouncing the opposition. But before I reveal my power secret, let me explain what I did as the chaplain of the Miami Dolphins.

The Eagles, Steelers, Oilers, Cowboys, and all the rest felt the impact of my secret weapon. Not one escaped. Before they put on the uniform, before an ankle was taped, before the helmet was doffed and they ran out onto the field, there was a heaviness that hung over them; a slight tendency toward poor timing, a clouding of the coach's mind.

They were foreordained and predestined to miss blocks, tackles, passes, and field goals. Shula got the credit. Moody was the cause.

Lest you think I am exaggerating, the facts are patently obvious. When the time came that I accepted the offer to become the pastor of the First Baptist Church of Van Nuys, California, an amazing thing happened. A close examination of every home game for the previous three seasons revealed that every team to whom I ministered my sermon . . . lost.

The first Sunday I didn't speak, the Dolphins lost!

I received a telegram from a "friend" of mine. It read: "Come back, Dr. Moody, please. We didn't know it was your lousy demoralizing sermons that paralyzed our opponents. We are prepared to double—even triple—your previous salary to return." It was signed "Coach Shula."

I could not return because of my high calling. But I did apply to the Raiders in Los Angeles. They turned me down. Look what happened to *them*! They fell from grace, lost games, and the coliseum crowd dropped off. Then they finally slipped out of town in the middle of the night and fled back to Oakland.

And to think—if they had only looked to me to preach what Shula called "those demoralizing sermons," to their opponents, the Raiders would now be dusting a shelf of Super Bowl trophies!

THIRTY-THREE

Billy Bartie's Hollywood Shorties

Perhaps the most enjoyable and most poignant experiences of my ministry were with two dear friends, Frank and Carole Law.

They were "little people," dwarves. (But don't dare call them "midgets"! Dwarves hate the appellation.) They will accept "little people." I learned more about sensitivity from Frank than I have from all the emphases on any race.

I first met Frank one Sunday at our morning worship services. I couldn't take my eyes off of him. The first sight of this diminutive person seized me because of his size—but there was so much more. He was a sartorially savvy guy, right out of GQ magazine.

Fifty-dollar ties, twenty-five-dollar belts, tailored suit and shirt, definitely an upper yuppie, with boomer written all over him. Frank was a successful young executive, a computer expert.

Urbane, sophisticated, knowledgeable, a witty conversationalist, full of jokes, he could bring you to the floor with laughter. *I* had better not say a word about his height; but he felt free to make all sorts of witty allusions to his size. It made you howl. It made you love him.

There were more facets to Frank's life and interest than one would ever dream. Michael Jordan would have been shocked that Frank was an outstanding basketball player.

You read it right, *basketball player!* Frank played with the Hollywood Shorties, a team coached by the famous little-person actor, Billy Bartie. After I survived the incredulity of believing that this tiny little man was a basketball star, I discovered that there was a great deal of seriousness to his devotion to the sport.

The Hollywood Shorties played teams from all over Los Angeles—and won most of their games! How could they defeat teams with players 6' 11", or even 5' 11"?

When I asked Frank that question, he replied, "Easy. We have one rule. After the toss-up, or when the ball comes off the backboard, it must hit the floor before it can be played; and when one tall player passes to another, it must be bounced instead of thrown directly from one player to another."

The man with the greatest personality of anyone I have ever known is John Myrick, a very best friend of mine for more than twenty-five years. John is a riot-going-somewhere-to-happen.

Six feet, six inches tall, he was an all-American basketball player from Howard Payne University, who played on the team that toured the world with just-retired senator Bill Bradley. John howled in laughter and glee at the prospect of playing the Shorties.

John was the director of singles at our church for several years, and today is a media rep for many of the stars and a quite successful businessman. John seized the opportunity to devour them, as he put it. An all-American is nothing if not confident.

You haven't met competition until you have played the First Baptist, Van Nuys, "Devourers" (a name he coined on the spot). The Shorties took John up on it.

Frank brought the entire team to church the Sunday before the big game. It was to be played in our gymnasium. It was an amazing sight to see the entire team on the front row of the church, about fifteen of them, all three feet tall—or less.

When the announcements were made by John, it was a thing to behold. John asked the entire team to come to the platform, then—in mock derision—he towered over them, roaring like Goliath roaring at tiny David.

The Shorties just stood there, with a knowing look on their little countenances.

"Just *who* do you think you are, coming to this church, acting as though you can play basketball! You haven't the chance of a Mexican hairless dog in a Wyoming snowstorm of even staying on the court with us." He was roaring, like a Cape Horn maelstrom!

"Do you realize that even our pastor once played for Baylor University? (He neglected to tell them that it was on the team that lost every game!) You are *nothing* but a bunch of Chihuahuas in a big dog show! We'll grind you midgets into being half as tall as you are now! When we get through with you, you will be able to walk under a door, without opening it!"

I was scandalized at John. What I didn't know was that John had obtained their permission to put on this charade.

The Shorties growled back at John, jeering and booing him, bobbing and weaving, dancing in and out at him. The congregation was in an uproar of laughter, and Bartie's bunch loved it.

When game time came, the gym was packed.

All of us on the team knew that we had to go easy on the little guys, just to make a game of it. Remember, there was just one rule that was different than regular basketball—every time a ball was passed, bounced off a backboard, or tipped off, *the ball had to bounce on the floor first.*

Little did we know that this was the Achilles' heel for us. If you will think about it, this rule made *them* taller!

Myrick was our captain, and—being the clown he is at a time like this—he was a riot of super confidence.

The tipoff went to one of the Shorties. He dribbled goalward.

Did you ever try to guard a guy two feet, five inches in height, bending over, and dribbling a ball below himself?

He passed the ball to another Shorties by bouncing it on the court.

Did you ever try to intercept a ball that was bounced from one player 2' 5" to another taller guy, who was 3' 1"? And there you stand 6' 3" trying to get *down* to where the action is. Before the night was over, all the tall guys were suffering from backaches, from bending *down*.

In regular basketball, when the Bulls play the Lakers, it is a game of UP. *Up* after the tipoff; *up* on defense, *up* to block shots, *up* to take it from the backboard. But *these* little wiseacres had changed the game from *up* to *down*.

A ball would hit the floor; and while these mastodons were bending down to get it, grimy little hands would zoom under you, grab the ball, and roar away from you, almost dribbling under the wood and while you were rising up so you could chase this fast-as-the-wind *elf*, he would be away and under the basket for a layup.

And they rarely missed!

They didn't simply win that night. Oh, no! They beat the tar, pitch, and turpentine out of us!

Years ago, the Washington Redskins were thrashed by the Chicago Bears 73–0 in a playoff football game.

That wasn't humiliation. The great Van Nuys Baptist–Hollywood Shorties game . . . now *that* was humiliation!

Myrick was subdued, speaking barely above a whisper, for at least a week. "I can't believe it—darned *midgets!*" he muttered.

Frank got tired of it, and said, "Come on, Myrick, grow down!"

There is a lesson in humility, designed to be an everlasting law of the universe. Don't ever brag that you are going to beat a short guy. He'll get you if it is the last thing he ever does!

THIRTY-FOUR

Footsteps in the Snowy Night

When I was a young minister, I received an invitation to journey to England and Europe to preach for Youth for Christ. I traveled with several wonderful young men, full of God and committed to winning postwar youth to Christ. Among them was Bob Randall, with whom I traveled most, a marvelous musician, a true Christian friend, a deep-in-the-Lord guy. And a lot of fun. Also, there were Billy Graham and Cliff Barrows, as unknown as we were at that time. I will never forget conducting meetings to help gain a large crowd in Nimes, France, for Billy and Cliff. I must have spoken twenty or thirty times, sometimes to ten young people and sometimes a hundred.

A discouraging impediment was the time the communists tore down Billy's signs for the Nimes rally. Boris Bessmertney, Claude Breaux, and I drove an old Peugeot all around Nimes, putting the signs back in place.

Another effective team was led by T. W. Wilson, now the chief associate of Billy Graham. "T" traveled with the "Couriers for Christ" quartet from Moody Bible Institute. Arnie Robertson, Bob Macmillan, Gil Mead, the pianist, and Vern Van Hovel.

It was quite a successful time for helping to fill the vacuum of the disillusionment of thousands of teenagers. This was especially true in Germany. Literally hundreds of them came to Christ, and across Europe today, most of these people—now senior adults—are faithful to Christ.

Billy Graham was a driving force. I now quip, "Billy and I were in Europe together, and we were totally unknown. Now, that's been reduced by 50 percent."

We preached in Paris, Rome, London, Hull, Leeds, Sheffield, Edinburgh, Glasgow, Amsterdam, Stockholm, Oslo, and scores of smaller towns. This was before the Iron Curtain was raised by the Soviet Union, but the Cold War was brewing rapidly between Russia and the United States.

One day Bob and I received an invitation to come to a home in Germany to preach in a house church. The only problem was that the home was behind the Iron Curtain. We had to take the responsibility if we were caught across the border in Soviet-occupied Germany.

We were young and felt invincible, as well as deeply committed to respond when persecuted Christians asked us to come and share Christ and His Word with them.

Our guide said we could only travel by night, and the nights were terribly cold. It would be about a ten-mile walk. We left about dusk, and it was a good three-hour walk in the snow. Our guide, Klaus Neumann, knew the way perfectly.

The moon poured its lovely silver down upon the hills and valleys as we journeyed in the crisp, cold, clear night. I well remember cresting a slope and seeing something that told me communism could not stand—that freedom would ultimately win.

At the top of the slope, I looked down into the beautiful night-white valley. There were thousands of footprints—thousands of them—all walking westward. Not one set of prints was walking toward the Soviet-occupied area. The only prints in the snow journeying eastward were ours. Thousands moving westward. Six footprints were *ours*, moving to the east, with the gospel! To a college student, aflame with youthful love for Christ, it was far more exhilarating than the night chill!

We had been walking for well over two hours with frozen toes and noses. Perhaps we were nearly there.

"HALT!" The voice was loud, authoritative.

I could see myself spending years in a Soviet prison. I thought of Mother, Dad, Doris, my little sister, Jeanne, and all my Baylor friends. The chill that ran up my spine was much colder than the night air. Who was it? What did he want?

It was a man in uniform, but I couldn't make out what sort it was. Our guide spoke to him, and the two of them walked away from Bob and me, perhaps about fifty feet. They must have talked for twenty minutes. Then they came toward us. Only the good Lord knew how frightened I was!

The man was wearing a faded German uniform. He wasn't Russian at all. He was a friend from the house-church who had come to show us the way. I never wanted to kiss a man before or since; but I certainly wanted to that night!

As we approached the house, with its warming lights shining, I heard the people singing some old German hymn. Their voices were so radiant, so filled with Christ. I was almost warmed by the heat of Christian joy.

We entered the living room, and there must have been fifty people jammed together. I could tell that they were toasty warm with the grand, large fireplace, and the shining warmth of their friendly faces. It wasn't long before we were thawed out and drinking down the good, hot apple cider. I learned later that they had been saving it for us. It was such a delicacy in an almost starving part of the world.

I spoke to them from the text, "Behold, how they love one another." I remember saying to them something they simply could not understand. I told them that Western believers were sometimes more prone to fighting each other over some doctrinal interpretation. I said that we should read it "Behold, how they club one another."

They were astounded. "Don't you Americans know that such actions are what paralyzed Christianity in Europe? Don't tell us of controversy. Tell us what Christ is doing in the United States!"

I was most happy to report that thousands of young Americans were turning to Christ, and hundreds of them were going into the ministry. I spoke to them calmly, but when I said hundreds were going into the ministry, they began to weep profusely. I found myself almost sobbing; but it wasn't because of what was happening in America. It was because I had fallen in love with the German spirit of joy in Christ.

I realized that it would not be long before all of these people would be harassed or imprisoned for their beliefs. They knew it also, but it seemed that they were wearing that prospect like a badge of honor. They seemed envious of the possible martyrdom of some, as though dying for Christ were something beautiful and God-honoring.

I later heard that they were scattered, some imprisoned; and I am certain that some of them died for Jesus. They were unfree young people who, nonetheless, were free in the Lord.

I spoke for over an hour, and they wanted more! Bob sang for an hour—and they wanted more! I preached another hour—and they wanted more!

Our guide interrupted the fellowship by telling us it was 3:00 A.M., and we had to be back across the border by daylight. A groan swept across the group. They began kissing us, hugging us, and promising to pray that American Christians would get right with each other. They warned that the same loss of freedom would come to America if we didn't repent of the division.

As I walked in the night light, I wondered whether I was walking from paganism, or toward it. I still have not decided.

The last thing a beautiful young girl said to me, with tears on her cheeks was, "I will always remember your coming; I will meet you in heaven!"

"Yes," another shouted, "in heaven! We will all meet together at your mansion!"

My mansion, I thought. *I will be the gatekeeper for that young girl's mansion.*

"We'll meet at *your* mansion. It will be larger!"

I could not hold back the tears.

They all live in my mind to this very hour, fifty years later.

Oh, God, teach our world that freedom always follows a Christ-honoring people!

THIRTY-FIVE

The Day Naomi Entered Heaven's Gate

Dedicated to Marshal McLuhan, who patiently explained "Hot and Cool" to me. It was a "thou" time I shall ever treasure.

Naomi Jingst, wife of Calvin, mother of Amy and Cindy, and friend of Jess and Doris, died this week.

I was honored, deeply honored, to participate in saying farewell, as well as to congratulate the family upon her graduation! The service was held at the St. John's United Church of Christ in Michigan City, Indiana.

I wrote a little poem to Naomi. It hit me about 5:00 A.M. the day of the funeral. A poem from Jess about Naomi for Calvin and Amy and Cindy and the whole family!

> I talked to God this morning
> in Michigan City
> About the loss of my friend
> Naomi.

He said, "She wouldn't want you
   to moan in pity.
Besides, I gave her to you, so
   you owe Me."
I talked to God this morning in Michigan City
About the PAIN of my friend
   Naomi.
He said, "Life there is hurtful and gritty;
But HERE IN HEAVEN, it's far
   below Me."
I talked to God this morning
   in Michigan City
About the Joy of my friend
   Naomi.
"She was always so happy and quite witty,
But here, wit and joy
   completely o'erflow
     me!"

WHAT I SAID AT NAOMI'S FUNERAL

First, I read the Twenty-third Psalm, then I made the following comments:

He is the Shepherd who leads, and He led Naomi to come to Him . . . and though it hurts—it's best.

We'll see that clearly, later.

The Shepherd leads.

We follow, not knowing *where*.

We follow, not asking *why*.

Because we know *Who*, We need not ask *how?*

Naomi went *through* the troubled waters. Now, she drinks from waters still. The water is from the pure river of the water of life that proceeds out of the throne of God (Rev. 22). She sees in it the reflection of her newly formed face. But she sees more. She sees Christ's face, looking over her shoulder.

Naomi went *through* the valley of the shadow of death, the name of the land in the deepening shadows at the very base of the mountain where Jesus was tempted.

There, the serpents and wolves lurk to attack the helpless sheep. She faces none of that now! We fear dark shadows, but shadows never hurt anyone. His rod will beat away the serpents and the wolves. His staff will pull us back to the main path!

She has walked through all that now. She is on the other side of the *shadow* in the glorious *light!* She is seated at the table set before her, laden with the fruit from the twelve trees of heaven (Rev. 22).

The fruit is shining in glorious greens, cherry reds, apple yellows, wine purples, and plum blues! She has been coronated with the anointing of the oil of joy! She has been energized because her cup of happiness is running over!

Goodness and mercy, like two faithful little dogs, follow her daily . . . and she happily dwells in the house of the Lord forever!

Did you ever wonder where people go after they die and are admitted into heaven? I have. And I made a study of it, because of Naomi's death.

There is only one way in: You must pass through the Jesus gate—the main gate—to get into heaven.

(There is another gate that I shall tell you about, but that is for later. . . .)

After entering heaven, the Bible says we are faced with twelve gates.

Describing the New Jerusalem, John writes in Revelation 21 that the city is a perfect square and each side is 1,400 miles long (21:16).

On each side, there are three gates: four sides equal twelve gates. To see how beautiful it is, read verses 18–27.

The listing of the gates are these:

St. Peter's Gate. This is the gate for all of us who love Jesus, but denied Him time and again, and have wept over our inconsistencies. After we enter that gate, we are purged from the guilt of our vacillation, the psychological self-hatred of it, and we realize that it is gone!

St. Andrew's Gate. This is the gate for all of us who have brought others to Christ, as Andrew brought Peter to Jesus.

St. John's and St. James's Gates. These are the gates for all of us who have misunderstood the purpose of power, have misused it, abused it, sought, plotted for it—and sinned to get it. There, you are purged and changed from power to praise!

St. Matthew's Gate. This is the gate for all who have misused money, obtained it by crooked means, used politics to secure money by the use of political power, and trampled people to seize it. You are purged of it and given over to praise God for that deliverance!

St. Phillip's Gate. For all who have a burning heart to carry the gospel around the world, as Philip did by riding with the Ethiopian eunuch.

Acts 8:24–40 reveals one of the most interesting stories of how, transcending all racial prejudice, Philip won the Ethiopian eunuch to Christ—thus sending him back to Ethiopia to found the Coptic Church, which now has ten million members.

St. Thomas's Gate. For all who ever doubted God, God's Word, His faithfulness, His presence. All doubt is purged, and you move from doubt to praise!

Straight ahead are the gates most of us pass through:

St. Thaddeus's, St. Simon's, St. Bartholomew's, and St. James's Gates. For all who feel small, insignificant, ignored, unused, abused, and unblessed. There are so many people like this that it takes four gates for them to enter the New Jerusalem!

But a question remains : Aren't there supposed to be twelve gates? What is the twelfth one?

There is no Judas gate. Or is there? (More later on that; but the question hangs.)

What is the twelfth gate?

St. Matthias's Gate. This is the gate of the overwhelmed, the greatly honored, the fearful.

You will find his story in Acts 1:21–26. Can you imagine what it must have been like to hear that you had been chosen to take the place of one of the apostles of Jesus? Fear, insecurity, and raw need must have crowded his psyche.

He must have been on his knees hourly, asking the Holy Spirit to fill him, enable him to take the hallowed spot.

This is the apostle of newfound responsibility, who understands humility, who cries out for help.

Is this your gate? Walk in it!

It is too terribly tragic that there isn't a Judas gate. Or is there? I believe there is a gate that leads to destruction, to hell. It is not located inside, past the Jesus gate, where the other twelve gates are.

If, when you come to the Jesus Gate to receive what He has in store for all who believe, and it is found that you have not received Jesus . . . then a hollow, echoing voice megaphones through the universe bouncing from one galaxy to another: "Depart from me, you worker of iniquity—I never knew you! *Go* to the Judas gate!"

THIRTY-SIX

The Upside-Down Plate

Many years ago, when Billy Graham and I were just young men in the ministry, he and the great Torrey Johnson invited me to come to Winona Lake, Indiana, to help formulate a strategy to try to win the youth of the world to Christ.

Winona Lake was a lovely retreat center. One night there, beside the lake, Billy and I prayed about the future of America, Britain, and Europe. It was 1945. The war had just ended. We were all so young, but breathlessly in love with Christ, just waiting, waiting for God's next step.

Years later, I can get out in the still of the night at Glorieta, look up at those dazzling stars, and wait and wonder about God's next step. He's about to do something incredibly cosmic. I know. I feel the same movement of His touch that I felt back in the old days by Winona Lake's shores. I asked God to give us places like that, where young hearts can pound out love for Jesus the way we naive, good boys did in the long ago.

At one service, Billy stood up and challenged us all to give to save the youth of the world. While Billy prayed, I felt the Spirit say, "Give all you have, Jess." I had thirty-two dollars, total. I gave it.

But how was I to get home? That was train fare back to Texas—and food money.

There was a lovely little man there by the name of George Bernard. He and I had become friends. He must have been eighty—and I was twenty. We had dinner together that final evening. But it was the last paid-for meal. "The Last Supper" I called it.

While I was sitting at the table with George Bernard, his friend, C. F. Wigle said something about a song Mr. Bernard had written; then he mentioned the name of the song, "The Old Rugged Cross." My mouth fell open. I had been talking all week with the author of the world's most beloved song, and he had never mentioned it to me!

They had a custom at the dining hall at Winona Lake. The plates were upside down, the old-fashioned way. After we prayed, we turned over our plates. When I turned over my plate, there were thirty-five dollars!

"C. F. and I were led to give it to you, Jess. Use it for Jesus."

It was there I learned that you can't give away money to Jesus. It always comes back—with God's little extra to boot!

God shall supply all your needs according to His riches.

THIRTY-SEVEN

The Little Man in the Lobby

Jesus spoke so often in dualities. Salt and light, eyes and light, two masters, love and revenge, rock and sand—and a score of others.

He dealt with one duality more than others: you and your possessions. He related it to the eye more than anything else. "If your Eye is generous, the whole of your body will be illumined" (Matt. 6:22 *Moffatt's Translation*). He is saying that if your eye—your whole way of looking at people and—is generous, then your whole personality will light up!

One of my favorite people is Alastair Walker, a glorious preacher from South Africa whose life has brightened everyone who meets him. He and I created a program, which later became known as "Key-73." We presented this to the heads of evangelism from a dozen different denominations at the Key Bridge Hotel in Washington, D.C.

I went into the lobby to pick up a message at the desk, and I noticed a rather small man seated across the lobby. His eyes were riveted on me. Wherever I moved, his eyes followed me.

Perhaps it is someone who has seen our services on TV, or maybe he is from West Palm Beach, I thought.

Whatever the case, he would not stop staring at me.

I walked across the room and faced him squarely.

He stood up from his chair, looked right through me, and said, "You are a fine-looking young man. May I ask you a question?"

"Of course."

"Do you know that every molecule in your body was made by, and for, Jesus Christ?"

"Yes sir."

"Then may I ask you another question?"

"Of course."

"Have you given them all to Him?"

"I am most happy to say that I have done that!"

"I have done that too! You may hug me!"

That was the day I met E. Stanley Jones, the great Christian missionary to India for forty years—and the man who came closest to reaching Mahatma Gandhi for Christ.

Do you know that Christ made every molecule in your body?

Have you given them all to Him?

If not, will you do so now?

THIRTY-EIGHT

Mudbound in the Goo of Ego

The word *search* is the word a Jew would use in cleaning his house before serving the Passover meal. It means, "Do the complete job of searching my heart." Do a good bit of detective work in my emotional nature to see if there is evidence of any misdirected road I'm taking, so I can get myself back to the main path that leads me into experiencing—right now—everlasting life.

A person who habitually chooses the evil to the good will never know who he is. Self-knowledge comes from forgiveness. Remember what Jesus said, "Except a man be born again, he cannot see the kingdom of God" (John 3:3, KJV). If you can't see the kingdom of God, you cannot know who you are. Self-understanding comes from God's love.

There are several Greek words for *love*. The two I want you to look at are *eros* and *agape*.

Eros is a love that is rooted in the object loved. I love that woman so long as she is beautiful. As her beauty fades my love will fade. I love that man so long as he can provide the security I need. When that security falters, my love will falter. That is eros love. I will love the object so long as it remains the object it was when I fell in love with it.

Then, there is agape love. Agape love is rooted in the subject who does the loving. When the beauty of the woman loved begins to fade, the subject loving her will not see the wrinkles but sees a beauty no one else can see. When he is not able to provide the security she needs, her secure love for him will not falter.

Eros loves because of what its object does; Agape loves because of what its object is. So, the sort of love with which you should love yourself is God's kind of love—agape love. This is the kind of love that will put up with your own weaknesses, blemishes, and failures. You will love yourself in spite of yourself.

Now, I want to tell you what self-love is not. Self-love is not an expression of ego. Erotic self-love is ego loving ego. When one fails, ego suffers—so love suffers. Agape self-love is understanding how God loves me and loving myself with that kind of love.

If, years ago, Muhammad Ali was serious when he proclaimed, "I am the greatest! I am the king of the world!" and he loved himself with erotic self-love, his ego would not love him now that he has been dethroned. This sort of self-love is totally destructive.

Neither is self-love narcissism. Narcissus loved Narcissus by looking into a reflecting pool and loving what he saw. Narcissistic lovers always have bad backs because they bend over backwards while walking past a mirror. He says, "Mirror, mirror on the wall, who is the fairest of them all—and you'd better get it right!" The love of self-beauty will falter when self-beauty falters.

Additionally, self-love is not self-will. That is why it does no good to say, "Come on, try loving yourself a little bit" to a person with a poor self-image. If he could love himself by his own will, Lord knows, he would have loved himself a long time ago.

God and His forgiving grace are the only sources of the self-love, agape self-love, you must have. This can only come when you stop trying to love yourself and let God's forgiving, cleansing, establishing grace do the job for you that you cannot do for yourself.

Then, how does self-understanding come about? You must hitch your idealism to the Word of God. Then you won't make Solomon's mistake and seek mere secular wisdom, the kind you can get at some secular school. Humanistic wisdom can only reach as far as humans go. If we are afraid of ourselves, we are afraid of others; for if we do not understand ourselves, we cannot understand others.

Your highest goal must be tied to the Word and the will of God. You must have priorities that coincide with God's Word. What is first in your life? Can you honestly find biblical agreement with your first priority? If so, you will love what is first in your life—because what is first in your life is an extension of yourself. If you, therefore, love what is first in your life, and it is in agreement with God's Word, you will love yourself.

"Seek ye first the kingdom of God and his righteousness and all these things [including self-love] shall be added unto you" (Matt 6:33, KJV). It isn't something you screw up your self-will and get. It is something that is added—by God—to you.

Add to these priorities having an imagination that is fired by the Word of God. David discovered it. "While I was musing, the fire burned. . . ." (Ps. 39:3, KJV).

If you are musing (meditating) on the Word of God, that Word becomes fuel, the Holy Spirit becomes the igniting fire that consumes the neurosis of self-loathing and narcissism of secular self-love.

This will protect you from the unreality that is constantly reinventing itself and reimagining the landscape. These kind of things undermine the confidence people have in you . . . making you a feckless fumbler, who stumbles because of walking in the eerie lowlight of secular self-congratulation.

You aren't mudbound in the goo of ego; you are freed up to get a panoramic view of all of life, including your own self-image.

THIRTY-NINE

"The Word of a Gentleman"

David Livingstone had a magnificent obsession with Africa. He was captivated by the fact, as he said, that there was the smoke from thousands of villages where people had never heard of Jesus Christ. To this, he gave everything he had to Christ—for Africa's sake.

What drove him most was the words of Jesus, "Go ye into all the world . . . and lo, I am with you alway, even unto the end of the world" (Mark 16:15, KJV).

He wrote in his Bible, "This is the word of a Gentleman of the most strict and sacred honor, so that's the end of it."

He gave everything he had to preaching the Word of that Gentleman and to fighting the Mohammedan-driven slave traffic to the United States. His last days in Africa are unbelievably wonderful.

An Arab had stolen his quinine. He was too far inland to send for more. People of "common sense" would have said to return rapidly back to more quinine—then return and preach more. But no, there was the drawing power of the smoke from a thousand Christless villages. He told the natives helpers to press on *inland.*

David grew worse. His feet too ulcerated to walk, the malaria fevering his brain, he babbled, "Smoke . . . go . . . Word of a Gentleman . . ." The native leader begged him to return. "No, there's another village just a mile or so farther . . . smoke . . ."

One night, they were sleeping in the jungle. The predawn sky was changing to grey light. The giant leaf of a *jububu* was filled with the night rain, and it snapped under the weight of the water, and spilled onto the native leader's face, waking him.

The faithful native peered into the grey dawn and saw Livingstone, kneeling, his dead eyes open and riveted onto "Lo, I am with you alway, even unto the end of the world." Scrawled right beside that verse were the words, "This is the word of a Gentleman of the most strict and sacred honor, so that's the end of it."

The natives cut out his heart and buried it in the jungle by a stream. His body was taken to London, where he was buried in Westminster Abbey, at the center of a room surrounded by the tombs of kings. On the stone, these words were placed: "It is the word of a Gentleman."

Let us, each and all, commit to that Gentleman's Word.

FORTY

The Headache That Changed the World

There was a hurting throb in Edward's temples that hot day. He was almost angry because the headache wouldn't stop using his brain as a giant drum to awaken and remind him of what an important day it was.

"But I can't go today!"

But, living in his memory was a vow, a commitment he had made.

"My head is killing me, but I said I would do it, so I will."

Edward wasn't a man to go back on his word. He had dallied in the past. A few years before, he would have made up some excuse—and stuck with it. But today, this wasn't just something one could laze out on. This, to Edward, was the most serious work in the world—so he would go.

As he walked down the hot street, he felt some better because he was nearing his goal. "Let me think. I forgot exactly where it is. Just past the foodmongers, then Goldbloom's Clothiers . . . there, there it is." He turned into the store, walked up to the gentleman at the front counter, and asked for his friend.

"Yes, he is in the back of the building."

There was a stockily built young man halfway up a ladder, counting the endless rows of boxes.

"Yessir, may I help you, Edward?"

"Yes, Yes. Thank you. I have come from town to tell you that the world has yet to see what God can do in and through a man totally dedicated to Jesus Christ."

There. He had said it. Perhaps too bluntly, but he had said it! Headache or no headache, he had said it!

The young man stepped down from the ladder, put his pencil in his pocket, put down his inventory pad, and turned squarely to face Edward. "Would you repeat what you just said?"

"I said, 'The world has yet to see what God can do in and through a man totally dedicated to Jesus Christ.'"

There, he had said it again!

The words burned deeply in the young salesman's soul. Then, he did an unforgettable thing. Edward was a little taken aback by the young man's reaction. He thrust out his hand and said, "Edward Kimball, by the grace of God I'll be that man!"

That was the day Dwight L. Moody became a Christian. Kimball and others helped him to grow as a disciple of Jesus—not just a Christian, but a *witnessing* Christian. He went on to start a Sunday School for little street urchins, a group that grew to be several hundred. Then, he became a preacher, a strong speaker for Christ. Later, he started evangelizing people on the streets, in the shops among the soldiers of the War Between the States, in hospitals . . . just everywhere. He vowed to witness to at least one person each day.

Finally, Dwight L. Moody became the man who took one continent in one hand and another continent in the other and he drew them both to Christ. He preached in massive evangelistic crusades; he preached for Spurgeon in the Metropolitan Chapel in London. He organized massive evangelistic crusades, designed so perfectly for witnessing by thousands at the World's Fair in 1898, that General Motors used his organization as a model of how a major national business should be operated.

But this story takes a most interesting turn, noted by few.

One day, during a Moody-Sankey Crusade, a troubled young man sat far out in the crusade crowd. The Holy Spirit took special notice of this bright, searching, questioning young person. When Moody gave the invitation, the young seeker received Christ.

His name was J. Wilbur Chapman. Chapman later became a great evangelistic force, preaching crusades across America. And with profound success. It is said that half a million souls came to Christ under J. Wilbur Chapman, the seraphic storyteller.

A dynamic young man was trying to find his way, having made a decision for Christ, but needing further direction and grounding. Billy Sunday was a professional baseball player and during the off season, he filled his time by working in the J. Wilbur Chapman crusades. He did everything, helping to set up giant tents, selling hymnals for fifteen cents, ushering during the services . . . and listening to J. Wilbur Chapman's great sermons.

Sunday had a marvelous memory. He memorized Chapman's sermons to the letter. Late at night Billy would, as he said it, "Put the athletics to the stories"—that is, he would act out, physically, the stories he had memorized so perfectly.

One day, he came up to Dr. Chapman and told him that he was ready to try preaching in an evangelistic crusade. Dr. Chapman, a gracious spirit, and a discerner of talent, told him of a small crusade in Ames, Iowa, which was very close to Billy's birthplace. Without hesitation, and with great gratitude, Billy seized the opportunity—but with one question "How long is the crusade, Dr. Chapman?"

"Eight days. You'll preach once a day."

That was exactly what Sunday wanted to hear. Because he had memorized exactly *eight* of J. Wilbur Chapman's sermons!

Billy Sunday was greeted at the train by a delegation of city, civic, and religious leaders.

"Dr. Sunday, we are most honored to have you in our city."

Dr. Sunday indeed! He wasn't even a practical nurse!

"Dr. Sunday, Dr. Chapman has told us that he is sending one of his most trusted and gifted associate evangelists for our crusade."

Associate evangelist!

"Chapman sure knows how to set a fellow up for a crusade. I hope these people don't find out that I'm just a hymnal salesman and chair arranger, just a little learner, trying to inch his way along."

Sunday's first crusade was a sensation. The crowds grew to monstrous proportions, and hundreds of people turned to Christ, as Billy acted out the Chapman stories.

He would slide on the stage, acting out the prodigal son's return.

"While he was away from Dad's house, with wild women, he wasn't *safe*. . . . While he was with those who made him a mark (sucker), he wasn't *safe*. But friend without Christ, I tell you, when the kid had gone down that *unsafe* road from wealth to the pigpen, decided to go back from the pigpen to Dad's house . . . and Dad saw him, Dad became a third-base coach, shouting and signaling 'Come on home! Come on home!'

"The kid barreled home like old Ty Cobb, with cleats flying.

"The devil didn't like this, so he was trying to throw him out at the plate.

"The kid slid in the dirt." *(Here Billy executed the perfect slide into home.)*

"The great Umpire peered in close at the kid who had been *unsafe* with wild women, *unsafe* with the pill bag, *unsafe* with the card shark, *unsafe* with the bunk artists, *unsafe* in the pigpen, and the great Umpire made the call in the cloud of dust: 'SAFE AT HOME!'"

The crowd went wild in that low-sensate time with no radio or TV. Their emotions were starved for a strong dose of gospel truth, and Billy delivered it as no one ever did before.

At the end of the eight days a committee of dignitaries came to him and announced that they wished to *extend the meeting another eight days!* Billy would have none of it.

"Why?" they pleaded.

"Because, boys, I've already preached more than I know!"

From here, Sunday preached to massive crowds all over America. A million people found Christ under his ministry—among them a young man by the name of Mordecai Ham.

Ham was a fervent pleader for the souls of men. He bobbed. He weaved. He hurled good, intellectually accurate information in a cognate dramatic and biblical manner.

This Billy Sunday convert was used mightily to reach masses of people for Christ.

His "Rimfire" meetings around Nashville literally saved the future for that great city, and established it as one of the headquarters for three national denominations.

One night in Charlotte, Mordecai Ham was preaching in a large crusade. Sitting in that crowd were two sixteen-year-old boys. When Ham extended the invitation to come to Christ, both young men were deeply convicted by the Holy Spirit, and they came to Christ.

One was Grady Wilson. The other was Billy Graham, the greatest Christian evangelist in the history of the world. It is estimated that more than five million people have come to Christ through his humble, Christ-exalting preaching.

And Grady Wilson was right at his side until his death.

I recall quite vividly bringing Billy to Texas in 1946 for his first time. He spoke on my broadcast, "Where He Leads," and the first time he preached was before an audience in Texas to the Baylor University Ministerial Alliance.

The next day, he and I went to San Antonio, where he preached at the First Baptist Church with Dr. Perry Webb and his associate, Billy Souther, a precious friend of many years.

We were walking down the street. Billy Graham and Billy Souther were walking ahead of us. I was walking with Herb Hoover, who was a great gospel singer with Billy. I asked Herb, "Who will be the next great evangelist to stir America for God?"

"He's walking right in front of you—Billy Graham."

Herb was right on target that day. I didn't know it *then*. I know it now.

As I read and reread this chapter, I see how God works mightily through tiny deeds of service.

Kimball won Moody, and a million people were won.

Moody won Chapman, and a half million souls were won.

Chapman won Sunday, and a million more.

Sunday won Ham, and a half million.

Ham won Graham, and eleven million came to Christ.

And a thought crashes through my brain like a cannon ball through a crate of eggs: *What if Kimball had yielded to that headache?*

FORTY-ONE

Dreams on Wings

Recently I assisted in preaching the funeral of a longtime friend, M. E. "Doc" Rinker.

Doc was the president and CEO for a great company, the Rinker Materials Company, headquartered in West Palm Beach, Florida. I was the pastor of the First Baptist Church in that city for sixteen years. Doc Rinker was a member and a great deacon in the church.

He started the company with one small truck, a willing, working body, and a heart full of dreams. That was in 1926.

There was never a more industrious young man, or more honest, in all of the Palm Beaches. The word got around that you could depend on Doc Rinker to do the job right, and if it wasn't done right, he'd do it again.

This paid off, to the degree that when the company was sold in 1990, the price was 650 million dollars!

There were about fifty employees who had been with the company forty years or more, and had faithfully worked day in and day out to make Rinker Materials a great company. I am not quite sure how he did it—maybe stock options—but Doc had arranged to make each one of those employees—including the janitor of his office—millionaires.

Doc and I were extremely close during those years together, and we had the ability to play jokes on each other, some of them quite scandalous!

When I founded Palm Beach Atlantic College, and was its first president, we didn't have two nickels to rub together. One Sunday, I stood in the pulpit and kiddingly announced that Doc Rinker was going to give eight million dollars to the college for the Rinker School of Business. I thought everyone knew I was jesting.

Many of the older ladies in the church bugged Doc by saying, "When are you going to give that eight million dollars to the college, as you *promised?*"

This went on for nearly twenty-five years.

One day, Doc gave the eight million, because he loved young people so much; and because—as he said—"I want you old women to leave me alone!"

The day we buried Doc, there was a groundbreaking at the University of Florida, for another Rinker School.

Doc received two eternal lives. One, in heaven with Jesus. The other in the faces of thousands of young people who benefited from his generosity.

Don't you want two eternal lives like that?

FORTY-TWO

Lord, Keep Me Below the Black Line

Rome, August 3, 1975

While visiting Rome, I was staying at the Cardinal Hotel. For some reason, I was in a state of almost total exhaustion, and I didn't go out with our tour group that day. My mind was filled with wonders that I desperately wanted to get down on paper. I prayed for God's guidance to cause my mind to sophisticate the accumulation of thoughts, images, and experiences of the past few days in Israel and Athens. The day before had been spent touring Vatican City, with all its wealth and opulence. My heart wasn't in it. I longed for the simplicity of the lifestyle of Jesus.

(Before reading this essay, prepare your mind and heart by reading Matthew 15:9, Mark 7:8–9, 13, and 1 John 2:3–8.)

The Talmud has a significant quote: "There is not a man but has his hour, nor a thing without its place" (Eruvin, 58).

Far south of Jerusalem, on the southwestern bank of the Dead Sea, rises a mountain so stark, so foreboding that the very sight of it sends a chill or thrill throughout your body.

It is called *Masada*.

Old King Herod was always jealous of the power of Rome—and its architecture. He decided to build a fortress and place of rest atop this flat-topped, massive, mind-boggling mountain.

King Herod-the-Paranoid, as archeologist Dr. James Strange and I dubbed him, came very close to making Rome a wee bit jealous by this one feat. It was a self-contained, isolated freak of nature, an accomplishment of a very freakish man.

When General Titus sacked Jerusalem in A.D. 70, 960 Jews fled to Masada to live atop the mountain, hoping to reside there in peace and freedom.

Who could reach them there? Only the most resourceful army in the world would attempt it . . . and Rome was the most resourceful army in the world. So, they attempted it.

It took them three years—and hundreds of lives—but they finally succeeded in climbing the mountain, burning the Masada gate, and storming the fortress. When the Romans came roaring into the Masada fortress, they were met with silence and no resistance.

All 960 of the people lay dead, except two elderly women who told what happened. Josephus, the Jewish historian, told how each family head, rather than face the Romans, hugged and kissed his wife and each one of his children, then took his own life. And then he lay down beside his dead family, and was slain by his friends. Finally, when there was only one man left, he fell on his sword.

When the cheering Romans stormed the gates, their cheers died out as they found 960 bodies, lying in orderly fashion, arranged by families. It was the most hollow of victories, devoid of glory.

"There is not a man but has his hour, nor a thing without its place."

That hour was in A.D. 73.

That place was Masada.

Today, young Israeli soldiers are taken to this mountaintop, where they are sworn in as officers. It instills a spirit in these young men, which creates the vitality of this dynamic little army. They who do not understand the swiftness of the victory of the Six-Day War simply do not understand Masada.

I was at Masada not long ago. From high atop the mountain, one can see from one end of the Dead Sea to the other. A spectacularly sensational view!

As the wind blew into my face, I tried to put myself in the place of those brave men and women. A few minutes of that sort of meditation caused my mind to become consumed with a curiosity to know the truth about this historic place.

I probed Dr. Strange concerning the real, sure-enough, bedrock facts about the customs, the terrain, and the architecture of Masada, this place that reeks of commitment.

It is so freighted with history that it is an archeologist's Disneyland. There were walls of an ancient bathhouse. While Dr. Strange was waxing eloquent about the bathhouse built by Herod-the-Paranoid, I noticed something quite unique about the walls: there was a wavering black line running along every wall, every edifice, every piece of standing architecture.

"Doctor Jim, what is the meaning of the black line?"

"All construction below the black line was here at the time Masada fell; all above the line is that which has been added later," Dr. Strange explained.

A bolt of electric insight crashed through my brain. "THAT'S IT!" I shouted.

"That's what?"

"That is what everybody who ever comes to the Holy Land wants to know: What is below the black line, and what is above it; what is sure enough, and what has been added since?"

Come to think about it, isn't that what everybody, everywhere, wants to know about everything? What is above the black line? What has been added that doesn't belong? What is below the black line? What is the original, basic sound truth of the matter?

What is sure enough, with no intellectual spit and polish, no varnish, no additives, no traditions, and no propaganda?

More agnosticism has been caused by people discovering that what has been called the original is, in actuality, not that at all.

While traveling through the Holy Land and Rome, I developed a little technique, which I used with those with whom I traveled. When we were told that something was the original site, method, or teaching—if I thought it was above the black line, I would hold my palm upward. If it sounded right, or accurate, I would hold my palm downward, signaling that it seemed right and reasonable—below the black line.

Illustrations:

"There are the original walls of Jericho."

Palms up! Above the black line. Reason? Modern Jericho is not where ancient Jericho was located.

"These can't be the walls!" said eight-year-old Bo Bradley, who was traveling with us.

"Why not?" someone asked.

"Because the Bible says the walls came tumbling down. If they were down, they wouldn't be up. Right?" Bo knew what was above the black line.

Another illustration:

"This is exactly where Jesus and His family lived when He was a boy."

Above the black line. Reason? No tradition, no history, no writing indicates where He lived in Nazareth.

Another:

"These are the exact streets, here in Jerusalem, where Jesus walked."

Above the black line. Reason? The original streets are thirty feet below the modern streets.

Another one:

"Peter spent twenty-five years serving in Rome."

Above the black line. Reason? Peter was not in Rome for more than one year—if ever. This is rather easy to prove.

Isn't it too terribly tragic that people think they must embellish plain, provable truth with the garnish of imaginings and reasoning? It isn't at all necessary.

Bare facts, below-the-black-line truth is startling enough, saving enough, without the spit and polish of fantasy and additives.

The place where Jesus was crucified, buried, and resurrected is so overlaid with architectural gaucherie that Jesus, who was the class act of all history, has to carry so much baggage that He is not allowed on the plane of believability.

Get rid of the baggage!

A worldwide movement to Christ, of historic proportions, will break the seals of the new tomb (man's foolish and unnecessary rewriting of history) and will awaken the longings that have long slumbered in humankind's hope chest.

Jesus is so easy to accept as the world's Savior, once one can see Him as He was and is!

Get rid of the overlay of stone, tapestries, gold, silver, mosaics, and fine wood work. Get back to the divine human nature of Jesus. Believe in His deity, which all Christians accept . . . and believe in His humanity—which most Christians accept *in principle.*

Many trip up when they begin to specify that Jesus went through normal bodily functions such as burping or hiccuping or—God forbid—being tempted by a beautiful woman!

Tempted, but never yielding.

He was "in all points tempted like as we are, yet without sin" (Heb. 4:15, KJV).

Get to that, and the sheer reality of it will touch the hearts of real men and women, as never before.

True, deep—though covered—belief, really wants to get below the black line.

Nothing below the black line offends anything but our sinful nature; everything above the black line deeply offends our need for an accurate sense of history, moral sensitivity, and spiritual responsiveness!

True Christians will do anything for that which is below the black line, and practically nothing for that which is above it.

But some churches are super-klutzy, clumsy about proving that they are below-the-black-liners.

I once saw a church that bore a huge sign: "FOUNDED, A.D. 33."

The ramshackled old building made you believe it!

Others claim to be connected by apostolic succession—that is, a lineage of leaders, who represent a historic, continuous chain, not one link of which has been broken since the time of Christ.

The Baptists, the Catholics, and others have tried to prove it to be true of them. It can't be done; but if you say it often enough, with enough fervor, and some dizzy documentation, you can get a following that you wouldn't believe! They strain every ounce of credulity to make it happen.

Some Baptists use an old, small book called *The Trail of Blood* to prove that they are the only ones who are connected—directly, unbrokenly, and historically—with the Christians of the first century. They get in bed with some strange birds to accomplish this marvelous feat.

Example: Some of the connectees believe that Jesus did not become the Christ, the Son of God, until His baptism by John the Baptist—and then, He was only adopted!

How far above the black line do you want to go?

The way to tell if your church is in line with the truth is not by apostolic succession, but by apostolic success.

If a church is doing *now* what they were doing then for the same reasons—to glorify Christ—then yours is a true church.

You have a direct, vertical, spiritual connection with Christ and the Holy Spirit. It makes no difference if you cannot prove a direct, horizontal line—as long as your vertical one is alive and functioning.

But don't we malfunction because we are constantly adding to biblical truth and spiritual reality, to cause the truth to conform to what we *want* it to say, rather than what it says?

Do some of us demand signs from the Lord that are more than what He wants us to have? When the disciples sought a sign of His coming, He refused, stating that the only sign to be given would be the Resurrection. Our Lord knew the nature of man to worship the sign instead of the Sign Giver.

We are so prone to put up a sign to honor the sign! Peter saw the transfiguration of Christ, and said, "Let's build three tabernacles!" There he was, wanting to put up a sign, honoring a sign. Our Lord is a bit skimpy about putting up signs because He wants the Resurrection to be enough—and it *is* enough!

If the cross cures the problem of sin, and the open tomb cures the problem of death, and the Holy Spirit cures the problem of sorrow . . . what further signs do you need?

Some people need tongues; others demand an inner light. Still others want Gog and Magog to refer to Russia so badly they can taste it. Others seek a wet fleece every morning. But, for me, the *fact* that Jesus died on the cross . . . and the *fact* that He isn't here in the tomb . . . and the *fact* that His Holy Spirit is here from the sky . . . are more signs than my thrilled soul can ever assimilate!

The good stuff is that every one of these facts is below the black line. . . . They're mine! And they can be yours.

Remember the quote I began with: "There is not a man but has his hour, nor a thing without its place."

Find your golden moment and wondrous "thou place" by coming to Christ *now!*

FORTY-THREE

"The Pilot of the Dragon"

Billy Tittle's handsome young face begged me, "Please, Doc, do what you can to get me on the staff at Glorieta. I want to get my life squared away with Jesus!"

I did what I could, and old Doctor E. A. Herrin let him in.

Billy's assignment was a high calling, running the "Dragon," which was the dishwashing machine at the dining hall.

That summer, Billy spent many nights on our front porch of "El Rancho Not-So-Grande," our little cabin. The night air was pierced by his infectious laughter, as he told tales about what the staffers were getting away with, and what girl he had his eye on, and a hundred things too numerous to retell.

"I am the lead pilot of the Dragon!" he said.

A few years later, helicopter pilot Bill Tittle—home on furlough from Vietnam—stopped by our parsonage in West Palm Beach to tell us he was headed back to "Nam."

"Dad and Mom Two" (that's what he called us—I loved that), I may not make it back; but if I go, I'll go straight to Jesus. I settled that up on your front porch at Glorieta. I can face that flak coming up at me, because I really met Him in those Glorieta hills.

My blood ran cold as he got into his car and drove away.

Twenty months later, a young lieutenant and I walked stiffly and hesitantly to the front door of the Tittle home. Lydia, Billy's mother, stood framed in the picture window, looking out in red raw terror at the news she was about to receive.

"Mrs. Tittle, I regret to inform you that your brave son, Billy Tittle, died heroically, on his 1,298th mission. . . ."

Just two missions short of coming home.

As I stood there, holding Lydia in my arms and feeling the absolute shaking to the depths of her soul, I looked out the picture window and saw little rosebuds popping out, and a happy little bird pecking around in the grass, and I remembered Billy's voice the last time I saw him.

"I'll go straight to Jesus, because I really met Him in those Glorieta hills." That is why the Glorieta and Ridgecrest staffers are so special to me.

FORTY-FOUR

Thumbs-up

Once, I was so far down the ladder, I called Job "lucky." I investigated how to reinvent my life; but I didn't want a new life that couldn't be patented. The quality of Christ's new life for you must be superior to the life you had before the big tragedy struck. That is *exactly* the promise Christ makes: "If any man be *in Christ,* he is a new creature: old things are passed away; *behold, all things are become new*" (2 Cor. 5:17, KJV, author's emphasis).

I love the way the Bible cooks. I love to hear those prepositions pop, those verbs vibrate, those adverbs advance, those adjectives advertise, and those nouns sing "The Hallelujah Chorus"!

I love those parts of speech in the Glory Story:

The Father *above* sent His Son *down* to be *with* us, so the Son could *live* and *die for* us, so we could be *like* Him, and the Son is *in* heaven *for* us and will come *to* us to take us *up* from here. The Father sent the Holy Spirit *to* us to be *for* us and *with* us and *on* us and *in* us and *through* us to sinners to *convict* us, to *convert* us, to *convince* us, to *fill* us, to *lead* us, to *change* us.

Man, this is the steak, the sizzle, and the French fries with the ketchup and the A-1 sauce thrown in!

Ever since Adam and Eve were evicted from their garden apartment, man has struggled to find new life; but man has concluded that it can't be done unless somebody helps Him. God sent that somebody; and that somebody is Jesus.

That restoration is part of the meaning of the word *Saviour!*

I promise that if you keep on running away from Him, you will get worse than you are now: more self-doubting, more lonely, more depressed, more emotional—or worse—more quiet, more frustrated, more frantic, more depressed than you are now. You will weave your own basket to make yourself a basket case.

You are a drowning person, and you are going to take some people you love down with you to the bottom of the sea of despair. That's not what you want! That's not why you were made!

You will live in *denial.*

Denial is a river of lies you tell others to explain why you are in such a puddle of tears and fears. It is a defense mechanism that protects you from anxiety over fear that everything is going to fall apart. You think everything is falling apart. You are falling apart, and everything will still be here after you are gone.

If you were gone, your wife would marry again, and her new husband would sit on your sofa, smoke your cigars, watch your television set—and, if you were to return, there would be more sorrow at your return than there was at your departure!

So, save your family and your home from the new guy by *becoming* a new guy in Jesus Christ! Show that future sucker that he can't have your stuff. Tell him, that's my stuff, and the new guy who will sit on my sofa will be me!

Your wife's going to get a "new guy" in her life—you're going to be that new guy.

She's going to love that new guy better than she did the old one. You'll become a new person in Christ, a person clear, cleansed, forgiven, reborn, washed in the blood, a new creature, with old things that hurt us gone; and new things that help us—active, vibrant, and alive in Christ!

My advice?

1. *Make a list.* Write down the things that need to be changed. If you can't think of anything, guess at it. You'll get it right every time! God gives us some words to help stimulate our memory—Romans 1:28–32.

2. *Don't water it down.* Call sin, *sin.* Don't say, "I had a little tendency toward rehypothecation." Say, "I am a liar." Don't say, "I exaggerated a little." Say, "I lied to you." Say, "God, I have sinned in 3-D and technicolor, and I am soul-deep sorry that I did it."

3. *Put Christ to the test.* Tell Him, "Here's my gunk. They say You don't make junk. I am a person, not a punk!" If you will provide the sinner, He'll provide the Savior!

   You give your life to Christ, and He will give you transformation, imputation, justification, propitiation, redemption, grace, forgiveness, righteousness, sanctification, glorification, and a three-tense salvation: *past, present, and future!* You'd better grab all this while you can!

4. *Accept Christ.* Embrace Him for what He claimed to be: your personal Savior.

5. *Confess Christ to others.* Walk down this aisle and personally confess Him in public who personally confessed you on the cross. It was you He was dying for while He hung there.

6. *Hold your head high.* You are a redeemed child of God. No more crying. You won't die. You're going to sing in the sweet by and by!

In the book *Foxe's Book of Martyrs,* there are hundreds of stories of people who died for their faith. There was a Christian pastor and fifty-five church members brought to the center of the Circus Maximus. Forty thousand people filled the large arena. Huge male, king lions were caged at the far end of the oval. Knowing what was about to happen, the Christians formed a circle of kneeling mothers, children, and fathers.

The crowd was cheering, full-voiced for blood. If Caesar gave a thumbs-up, the lions would be released. He taunted the crowds by alternately moving his thumb up and down, then dramatically locked it in an upright position.

The pastor prayed a never-to-be-forgotten prayer. "O, God, help us to die a death so glorious that we, even in our deaths, shall be a living-sacrifice testimony for our risen Lord!"

The crowd cheered, as the lions did their deadly work. In my mind's eye, I see the martyrs looking up . . . when suddenly, out of the clouds came a nail-scarred hand, giving them . . .

. . . a thumb's-up!

More Club Sandwich

If you liked *Club Sandwich*, and you have a story to tell, I'd love to hear from you. I would like to collect additional *Club Sandwich* stories of inspiration, encouragement, and just plain fun. If you have a great story, please send it to me at:

Jess Moody — Club Sandwich
c/o Southwestern Baptist Theological Seminary
P.O. Box 22000
Ft. Worth, Texas 76122